SIR ALAN SUGAR
The Biography

SIR ALAN SUGAR

The Biography

CHARLIE BURDEN

JB

JOHN BLAKE

Published by John Blake Publishing Ltd,
3 Bramber Court, 2 Bramber Road,
London W14 9PB, England

www.johnblakepublishing.co.uk

First published in paperback in 2010

ISBN: 978-1-84454-891-0

British Library Cataloguing-in-Publication Data:

A catalogue record for this book is available from the British Library.

Design by www.envydesign.co.uk

Printed in Great Britain by Bookmarque Ltd, Croydon, CR0 4TD

1 3 5 7 9 10 8 6 4 2

Papers used by John Blake Publishing are natural, recyclable products
made from wood grown in sustainable forests. The manufacturing
processes conform to the environmental regulations of the
country of origin.

CONTENTS

PREFACE

The British business world had never known anything like it. It was April 1987, and the lecture hall at the City University Business School was full of young budding business giants, and established financial analysts from the City itself. They were about to be given an entertaining lesson in how to make it in business by a man who was already a multimillionaire, having just turned 40 a matter of weeks before. It was to be a charismatic, direct and honest performance. Most of all, though, it was to be a truly instructive evening, one that will no doubt have served all those present well in their personal quests. Indeed, it's fair to say that the speaker was not so much going to give them a wake-up call, as chuck a bucket of ice-cold water over them.

'The priority in life is to keep an eye on the business and not to get lured into the social high life, being exhibited around by the groupie-type poseurs who wish to be seen with the new blue-eyed boy,' he told the aspiring entrepreneurs. Were any of those youngsters dreaming of working for the man in front of them in the future, they were given a succinct account of what that would entail. 'In our company we attract people who either catch on very quickly or they last two minutes. When they catch on, they understand the entrepreneurial flair of the company and see their colleagues using innovative ways and methods to achieve their tasks, not conforming to the standards that are written down in the books, but by cutting corners, taking a few risks.' He added that 'we don't want any corporate wimps'. Some members of the audience shuffled somewhat uncomfortably in their seats.

Turning to his own personal image, he said, 'For some reason, I have been called a barrow boy. I would take great exception to that if my ambition in life was to be seen daily at Annabel's with Lord and Lady Beseenwith. However, in a way, marketing is just like a stall in Petticoat Lane. Frankly, it is no different. The owner of the stall is offering his or her wares. The sales pitch, albeit very rural and loud, is no different than some high-cost advertising agency may apply.' He went on to outline more of his personal business manifesto, pouring more scorn on corporate culture, on 'up-market yuppies' and 'hi-tech ramble'.

Once a company has created a winning product, he said, there is no room for complacency or patting oneself on the back. He said he had witnessed this many times in his industry: a bit of success leaving a firm 'feeling their boat has come in and nothing can topple them from the Cloud Cuckoo Land they are in'. Instead, 'you knock the living daylights out of the thing, as opportunities come very seldom and you make the most of things when the opportunity allows'. By this time, it seemed he had the audience in the palm of his hand.

He even found time to attack other companies, and had no respect for big names in doing so. Once more, he told it as he saw it. 'In the USA we sold goods to Sears,' he snarled. 'The mighty Sears, where the left hand does not know what the right hand is doing. They obtained the marketing rights to our word processor, ordered shiploads and stored them in a warehouse in stacks nearly as high as the Sears Tower in Chicago.' He then outlined how he felt Sears had taken its eye off the ball and let Amstrad down. 'This is a case of big not being beautiful,' he snapped. 'The Sears Tower has 100-odd floors and I think they have that many layers of management.'

He concluded the speech by summing up the culture of his company. In doing so he managed both to mock the overelaborate slogans many large corporations used, and to be humorously to the point about his own company's philosophy. 'Pan Am takes good care of you. Marks & Spencer loves you. IBM says the customer is king. At Amstrad, we want your money!' He stepped down from the podium to spectacular applause. *The Times* roundly praised his performance in the following morning's edition, under the headline 'A Recipe for Sweet Success'. It had been a memorable performance. The following year, City University awarded him an honorary degree.

Several years later, he would once more spell out a basic business philosophy. 'We're interested in the mass-merchandising of anything,' he said. 'If there was a market in mass-produced nuclear weapons, we'd market them too.'

Two decades later, he would deliver his own business wisdom in a similarly forthright style to aspiring millionaires on a television show, by which time the fortunes he had made as a 40-year-old would seem small change.

INTRODUCTION

'Is there a Sugar "brand"?' Sir Alan Sugar was once asked. 'Yes, Tate & Lyle' was his impatient reply.

He is not a man keen on overt analysis. His most memorable lines of self-description on *The Apprentice* concerned more what he was *not*, rather than what he *was*. 'Mary Poppins I am not,' he told contestants, before adding, 'I don't like liars. I don't like cheats. I don't like bullshitters. I don't like schmoozers and I don't like arse-lickers.' However, one thing that he told them that he definitely *was* was a one-off. 'Don't start telling me that you're just like me, because no one's like me; I'm unique,' he declared. There was of course always plenty of theatre and bravado on both sides of the boardroom table during *The Apprentice*, but this 'unique' claim was not without merit. Such is the breadth of areas that Sugar has worked in that his life has proved to be something of a one-off.

But who is Sir Alan Sugar? To some, he is the man who has become synonymous with the phrase 'You're fired', thanks to the smash-hit success of *The Apprentice*. To others, he is still associated with football, thanks to his eventful time in charge of Tottenham Hotspur Football Club. Then there is his property empire and his private-jet company. Of late, he has also become something of a political figure, working alongside Gordon Brown on several projects. And, of course, Alan Sugar is the man who rose from a humble beginning in the East End of London to form the electronics company Amstrad, and go on to amass a fortune that runs comfortably into the hundreds of millions of pounds.

With an almost snarling determination, Sugar has built his business empire and personal wealth in breathtaking style. His is a truly, classically inspiring tale of ambition, energy and brainpower. On occasion, he has described himself as a 'salesman', and it is true that Sugar has an uncanny ability to sell. Even at school, his headmaster had noted, and been bowled over by, Sugar's powers of persuasion. If your life depended on a sale being made, you'd want Sir Alan to be the man knocking on the front doors. However, there is so much more to Sugar than a simple salesman. He has an extraordinary eye for all aspects of business, from planning to the legal side and far beyond.

He also has a refreshing honesty, and a wonderfully straightforward, yet evocative turn of phrase. When asked to describe the person who bought his early computer models, he said, 'He looks at this thing, with its whacking great big keyboard and a monitor, and he has visions of a girl at Gatwick airport where he checks himself in for his holidays. And he thinks, "That's a real computer, not this pregnant calculator thing over there called a Sinclair."' A good description: what it lacks in romance it more than makes up for in honesty and focus. To know your market is a key business asset. Sugar knows his like the back of his hand. Further honesty was apparent when he gave another lecture in 1987, and told his audience how he first learned what P/E ratios are. To the uninitiated, P/E stands for 'price-to-earnings', and represents the ratio between the share's price and its actual earnings. However, as Sugar explained, he was somewhat confused when he had been asked in 1979 what his P/E ratios were. 'The last time I heard the expressions "PE",' he recalled thinking, 'I was at secondary school and it meant physical education.' So, when he was asked what Amstrad's P/E was, he replied, 'Twenty press-ups every morning.' He would soon learn what all this jargon meant, though, and, in doing so, show the City experts just who was boss.

Just as Sir Alan has an incredible sense of business, so does he have a refined sense of timing. It was Andy Warhol who said, 'Making money is art and working is art and good business is the best art of all.' In 21st-century Britain, the entrepreneur has assumed a whole new wave of glamour. Previously, young people mostly dreamed of becoming the next rock star, movie actor, supermodel or footballer. To them, the thought of becoming a millionaire through good honest business graft was not as appealing as these more glamorous routes to riches. However, thanks to a raft of new television shows in which the worlds of business and reality television are wonderfully intertwined, the entrepreneur has become a far more admirable and – whisper it quietly – sexy figure! Shows such as *Dragons' Den* and *American Inventor* have become hugely popular and the multimillionaires who star on these shows have become almost as famous as rock stars. As one of Britain's most brilliant businessmen, it is quite fitting that Sugar should have been at the forefront of this new trend with his acclaimed popular television series *The Apprentice*.

And who else could have done it? Would Rupert Murdoch have been able to charm television audiences the way that the Amstrad man has? Does Richard Branson possess the necessary snarl-ability to be at the helm of a show such as *The Apprentice*? Meanwhile, the Dragons of the Den are all immensely enjoyable television figures, but they work only as a team. None has sufficient individual charisma to work on the screen alone, as Sugar does. When they have tried to go it alone – as Peter Jones did with the ITV show *Tycoon* – they got harsh reminders that they do not have the Sugar-factor, and so they have had to return to the successful formula of teamwork, in *Dragons' Den*.

All the same, there was no doubt that enterprise had become sexy and Sugar has seen this trend coming a while back, saying, 'The UK is poised for more enterprise. Not everyone can be an entrepreneur, but people have a fixation that Shell or BP are the backbone of the country. They're not. The actual backbone of the country is Fred with six employees in the garden centre, or in the garage. They're the ones who employ the majority of people in this country. Being employed in the old-fashioned way isn't that available any more. People have got to start thinking about doing things for themselves.' Just as he has caught this cultural trend brilliantly, so has Sugar managed to reflect in many ways the prevailing political climate that he is operating in. As he rose to prominence in the 1970s, he was, in many people's eyes, the ultimate Thatcherite, her vision personified. Here was a hungry young businessman who was willing to slog hard, take risks and shake up restrictive business practices in return for success and financial riches. No respecter of any bureaucratic nonsense or establishment figures, Sugar wanted to get to the top on his terms – and fast.

'There's a new breed of person coming up – the likely lad,' Sugar said with a smile during the Thatcher years. 'You see it in the City and everywhere. It's no longer Mr Heathcote-Smythe's son who's getting the job.' No wonder, then, that, rather than becoming part of the establishment, Sugar was dubbed as part of a 'disestablishment'. No wonder, then, that he received praise from the Thatcher administration. Lord Young, who was Secretary of State for Trade and Industry, said, 'He's one of a new breed of British entrepreneurs. I would like to see people like that as role models for young people coming into business. I want people to say, "Damn it, if he can do it, I can."'

Not that Sugar was entirely reciprocal. He insists there were never any barriers to his progress, under Labour or the Conservatives. He was also keen to avoid lazy generalisations, such as making the 1980s the decade of business. He believes that people are born the way they are, and they continue to be the way they are beyond decades. However, it remains the case that Sugar's ascent coincided neatly with that of Thatcher's, and that many saw him as a product of her times.

However, come the 21st century and the aftermath of Tony Blair's reign, Sugar again chimed with the political climate of the hour when he became a close confidant of Labour Prime Minister Gordon Brown. The new PM appointed Sugar to a business leaders' council. 'Let me tell you, this fellow is no mug,' said Sugar. He had long understood that the Labour Party would have to change if it was to retake power. 'The Left cannot be as our fathers would remember it in the old days. If the Labour government comes in, their policies will have to be virtually the same.' These remarkably prescient words were spoken more than seven years before Tony Blair, New Labour through and through, came to power.

Sugar started in business young, and his tender years would surprise many as he took the business world by storm. When he made his first business trip to Japan at the age of 21, the Japanese businessman with whom he had been dealing by Telex asked him whether he had come with his father. He couldn't get his head around the fact that he was dealing with a 21-year-old businessman. Once he'd made it, Sugar had no such anti-youth worries. Speaking of a female employee whom he hired at the age of 19, he said, 'She is mustard. Unbelievable. I'd match her against any businessman in the world. Personally, I would trust her with all my money.'

Needless to say, he's a canny operator. An early business trick of Sugar's – and one that was to remain for some time – was to lure customers into stores by advertising low-price or 'lead-in' products, and then make sure that next to the cheap product was a superior and more expensive version. 'The salesman "Dixonises" them,' said Sugar of how this would play out at his favourite retailers. 'He jumps on them and says, "Well, that one is the all-singing, all-dancing, more powerful, double-cassette, blah-de-blah." Nine times out of ten the customer will pay it off on credit, which works out at £1 a month more for the better one. The truth is we advertise the target lead-in price products, knowing that they will often end up being the lower sales.' Indeed, not only did Sugar have a strong grasp of what went on in stores such as Dixons, but he also had an intensive relationship with the retailers. Someone who sat in on a meeting between Sugar and Dixons said, 'These were not meetings where you would want to talk unless you had to because you would get ripped apart – by your own side if not the other. They were fighting over volume and percentage points for hours and hours.' The air would turn blue, and desks would be thumped. However, the same eyewitness said that, after slagging each other off throughout the meeting, often for hours on end, Sugar and the Dixons people would then step outside the meeting room and laugh about the whole thing.

Because, contrary to how he might come across on *The Apprentice*, Sugar is not a grumpy man. For the sake of making good television, his grumpy demeanour has been a major selling point for the show. True, he would not claim to be the most smiley man in the world, but those closest to him speak of a witty, generous and light-hearted man who is a million miles from the grump of *Apprentice* boardroom fame. However, the demands of television producers dictate that a moody and fearsome Sir Alan will make far better viewing on a reality show, so that is the side of him that is emphasised. 'What you see on screen is me, there's no question of that,' Sugar said. 'But it is the side of me the BBC chooses to show. There is more light-hearted banter, which hits the cutting-room floor because it doesn't put bums on seats. It's a one-way portrayal, not the whole of me.'

There are wider issues at play, too, in this image that has built up around him. When it was once pointed out to him that, in publicity photographs, he was traditionally pictured with a somewhat unhappy expression on his face, Sugar explained the thinking behind this tactic. He said that he'd been advised that, if there are photographs of him smiling in circulation, then should any of his business ventures go bust, leaving people out of work, you could guarantee that the newspapers would run the story with a photograph of him smiling or laughing.

Returning to those fuming Dixons meetings, and their humorous, peaceful aftermath, this shows that, despite his grumpy image, there is something special about Sugar's personality that means there is a far warmer undercurrent beneath the gruff front. Many Amstrad staff at one point were perceived to be imitating the direct-talking style of their leader. But, according to one retail contact, they got only half of the impersonation right. 'They imitated his aggressiveness, the most obvious side of his character, without having the intelligence to know that beneath it was a very perceptive, humorous, intelligent guy.' As an Amstrad insider put it, when Sugar told customers to 'bugger off', he did so with a twinkle in his eye. It was all part of the theatre.

Sugar, when asked for further reason for his sour

reputation, pointed to the unpleasant experiences he had in the football world during his time at Tottenham Hotspur. 'I think the poor reputation I had, sometimes deservedly, of "needing a charisma bypass", as someone once put it, was brought about by the horrible people that I had to deal with in that industry,' he said. 'It made me a very tight and protective person, not wanting to speak to anybody, thinking everybody's got an angle, everybody's out to try to get me. So I think coming out of that environment has released in me a much better person. I used to be quite a good joker and enjoy having a laugh but a lot of my friends said to me, "Since you've been involved in bloody Tottenham you've changed." I did. It was a wasted ten years of my life. It was a problem given to my family. No one deserved it really.'

There was indeed much less to smile about than he would have hoped for during his time in football. In 1991, he became chairman of Tottenham Hotspur FC and it was to prove a controversial time. True, he made many friends in the game but there were plenty of fallings-out, too. He remains defiant about those who have badmouthed him. 'Oh, do me a favour,' he snapped when asked about some less than kind words a footballer had said about him. 'Listen to a fucking football player? Will you get real? I don't know why you're wasting your breath talking about what a fucking football player says. They're scum, total scum. They're bigger scum than journalists, don't you understand?

They don't know what honesty or loyalty is. They're the biggest scum that walk on this planet and, if they weren't football players, most of them would be in prison, it's as simple as that.' This was, to borrow and adapt a football term, route-one talk, but he hadn't finished. 'Do not believe a word that comes out of their mouths. All they're interested in is themselves. Totally themselves! What money's in their pocket!'

This sort of language shows both his streetwise nature, and the strength that has allowed him to succeed. However, 'scum' footballers are far from the only obstacles he has faced on his road to riches. Jealousy has proved to be just as formidable an opponent. For, unlike America – which was the birthplace of the *Apprentice* series with Donald Trump as Sugar's forerunner – it seems Britain remains a country with a virulent strain of envy in it. The old comparison that when British people see a man driving a Rolls-Royce they sneer at him while when American people see a man driving a Rolls-Royce they cheer him stands as strong as ever in the 21st century. As someone who has done better than most with his life, Sugar is probably all too aware that with success comes envy.

However, it is to be hoped that the interest in shows such as *The Apprentice* and *Dragons' Den* will lead to a more balanced way of looking at successful businesspeople. Could it be that, in the future, British people begin to view those who make a success of their lives with admiration, and also with a curiosity: how can we learn from these people so we too can raise ourselves up? Could it be that this change has already begun to happen, and that Britain is already a far less resentful nation? If so, it would be partly thanks to Sugar, who helped kickstart the country's newfound respect for the businesspeople. Another factor that has helped bring around this change is the growth in 'you can do it too' self-help/business books. More and more millionaires are sharing their secrets, and encouraging people to try to follow their example and emulate their success. Dragons Peter Jones, Duncan Bannatyne, James Caan and Theo Paphitis are among the high-profile men to follow this publishing path. However, the shelves of your local bookstore are straining under the weight of books that promise to turn the mere mortal into the millionaire. As for Sugar, he's been generous with advice and support since long before it became fashionable or profitable. Not that he is a fan of business self-help books. 'I've never been a great believer in [them],' he said. 'I am a firm believer that, if you've got what it takes, you'll have a feeling in your gut, a hunger in your belly – and you'll know you want to be your own boss.' But those who have interviewed him, or simply those who know him, often tell stories of how he offered them, or those close to them, advice on how to get ahead in business. He has also returned to his school in Hackney to give encouragement and advice to today's pupils. Never one to kick the ladder away, Sugar has instead held that ladder firm for those who are trying to climb it.

Do not let his boardroom snappiness fool you: when the time is appropriate, Sir Alan is a man of kindness and generosity. He is a man of charity, too. As with some other wealthy and successful men, he regularly gives his time, expertise and money to fine causes. For instance, he donates to Jewish Care, a prestigious charity that looks after the elderly, frail, sick and vulnerable members of the Jewish community across London and the southeast with an enormous range of services and activities. In 1994, he donated £1.1 million to an old people's home in Ilford. The valuable work of Jewish Care has drawn praise from some fine quarters. For instance, former Prime Minister Tony Blair said, 'Jewish Care is not just Jewish values in action: it is actually the best of British values in action. You can be really, really proud of the work that you do.'

Sir Alan can also be proud of the work of the Alan Sugar Foundation. To take the accounts from just one year: it donated £297,000 to Redbridge Jewish Youth and Community Centre, and £150,000 to the United Synagogue Educational Trust's Redbridge School. Other gifts included £50,000 to Jewish Care, £25,000 to the Ravenswood Foundation, £10,000 to the Jews' College, London, and £5,000 to the National Youth Theatre. He virtually single-handedly saved Chigwell Synagogue from a debt of £200,000 by cleverly investing money and paying the interest, tax-free, into a charity set up for the synagogue. When the debt was paid off, he reclaimed his capital.

Even within the strictly business sphere, Sir Alan has shown a remarkable ability to put the company's interests ahead of his own. For instance, in the mid-1980s, Amstrad's profits were getting higher and higher, thanks to the company's successful computer operations. His financial advisers were urging him to increase further the level of the dividends paid out to Amstrad shareholders. Taking this step, he was told, would silence those in the City who were critical of Amstrad. He was having none of it, despite the fact that, with a shareholding of nearly 50 per cent, Sugar himself would have enjoyed a colossal personal payday had he followed their advice.

Similarly, in July 1985, Amstrad ran its first share-option scheme for employees. Many companies offer such schemes to their staff, as it's a good way of rewarding loyalty and encouraging hard work. However, few offer share options as widely within their walls as Amstrad did. Roughly one in ten of the staff from around the world, from directors right down to the most junior staff, was included. In total, 11.551 million shares were offered and the dividend three years later was to the value of around half a million pounds each. At the next annual general meeting, institutional investors expressed their disquiet at the level of generosity Sugar had shown. He brushed off their criticisms, and stood by his decision.

Even on a personal level, Sugar has shown loyalty to his staff. For instance, it seems he even helped one senior employee save his marriage.

He doesn't simply put his money where his mouth is, then: it seems he also invests his time. 'I personally believe you have to plough something back,' he said of the talks he has often given to young business students. 'It's the easiest thing in the world to write out a cheque, and of course that just deals with your conscience. I feel I go beyond that by actually wanting to get involved at a grassroots level. I talk to young people about enterprise and try to share with them how I made it and how they might be able to make it. I go anywhere within reason once a month, because they are an audience willing to listen.'

Something that Sir Alan can be – and is – proud of is his close and loving family. Far from his relatives being a mere sideshow in his life, he has made them his priority and far more important than his businesses. Asked for advice about how to make it to the top in business, he said, 'Put your loved ones, not your profit margin, centre-stage.' It is certainly advice that he has followed closely himself. He married his wife Ann in 1968, and those close to the Sugars speak of her with enormous warmth, respect and fondness. As does her husband. 'Ann is respected by everyone,' said Sugar proudly. 'She is the opposite of me but we complement each other and she can read me like a book. She knows when I have a lot on my mind and is happy to let me sit watching TV while I wind down. Sometimes when I get home on a Friday night my head is still pounding with the problems of the week.'

A family friend said, 'She's very much the family's anchor and Alan's personal anchor. They are still very close and loving with each other, which adds to Alan's strength as a businessman.'

Just as Sir Alan is a loving husband, so too is he a devoted father. Sometimes, the children of the rich can become greedy brats, but Sir Alan is justly proud of how grounded and level-headed his children are. 'I wanted them to see how the rest of the world live, to realise they have a privileged life,' he said a few years ago. 'I think they are all fairly well balanced. Ann and I wanted them to grow up with the same values that we had. I figure, once they've got past a certain stage and they're not out beating up old ladies, then you've won. They are really down-to-earth, nice people, don't sling their weight around. They've never been the Ferrari-driving, cocaine-sniffing, party-going type. They've got the right values.' Summing up the relationship between family and business, he said, 'You want them both settled. A happy balance. I was brought up with true family values. We were poor but we had standards. And my wife Ann came from a similar background. That's why we've been together 37 years.' And, in 2008, they held a lavish celebration of their 40th wedding anniversary surrounded by friends and family, the most important thing to them both.

INTRODUCTION

Throughout his career, Sir Alan has received plaudits and awards for his business work. He was voted the *Guardian*'s Young Businessman of the Year in 1984, at the age of 37. The crowing glory came when he was knighted in 2000, for services to business. He said, 'I think it shows how someone can start from a humble background and go on to be very successful. It is just a great shame that my mum and dad can't be around to see what happened.' A shame indeed, for the story of 'what happened' with this man's incredible life is gripping and inspiring.

This, then, is the incredible story of Sir Alan Sugar. The rags-to-riches story of how this incredible man moved from his East End childhood boiling beetroots for the local greengrocer, to his knighthood and seat at the table of former Prime Minister Gordon Brown. It covers all the drama, excitement and inspiration as he amasses an estimated net worth of £830 million and a place in the *Sunday Times Rich List*. Along the way, it proves handsomely that, when he boasted to *Apprentice* contestants that he is 'unique', he was – to use an apt term – very much on the money.

CHAPTER ONE
YOU'RE SIRED!

With the dark shadow of the Second World War still cast over the planet, 1947 was still an eventful year. The future Queen of England, Princess Elizabeth, married the Duke of Edinburgh, a crashed UFO was found in the desert in Roswell, leading to decades of speculation among conspiracy theorists and alien obsessives, and the United Nations General Assembly voted to partition Palestine between Arabs and Jews, a move that resulted in the creation of the State of Israel. There were some notable births that year, too, including pop stars David Bowie and Elton John, as well as future US politicians Hillary Rodham Clinton and actor-cum-politician Arnold Schwarzenegger.

And, on 24 March 1947, Sir Alan Michael Sugar was born in Hackney, east London, a man who was to become not just an immensely successful businessman, but also a television star, generous charity benefactor and all-out national treasure. It was a difficult birth and, in the end, he was delivered via caesarean section at the Hackney Hospital. He was the fourth child that Nathan and Fay's marriage produced, joining twins Derek and Daphne, and eldest sister Shirley in the clan. There had been shock in the Sugar household when it was discovered that Fay, then 38, was pregnant, as it had been a full 11 years since her previous child was born. After the Caesarean birth, Fay spent three weeks recovering in hospital, and she recalled that her newborn son was suitably bossy and noisy from the start.

One of London's most famous boroughs, Hackney was a strangely suitable surrounding for this future business giant's first steps in the world. A rough-and-ready yet charming and charismatic area, it is much like Sugar himself. Other celebrities to have been born in, or lived in, Hackney, include the star of the *Carry On* films and *EastEnders* Barbara Windsor, actor Ray Winstone, Ronnie and Reggie Kray, footballer Ron Chopper Harris, and *X Factor* star Leona Lewis. It is fitting that the borough has such a star-studded alumni, as it also has many cultural attractions, including the Hackney Empire theatre, which Sugar has played a large part in supporting. He is now a patron of the plush, charming theatre. Built on Mare Street in Hackney in 1901, this Grade II listed building has played host to such luminaries as Charlie Chaplin, W C Fields, Stan Laurel and Marie Lloyd. During his smash-hit television series *The Apprentice*, Sugar has regularly built tasks around the Hackney Empire, bringing both attention and funds to this national institution.

So what was the future tycoon like as a youngster? Sugar was reportedly a quiet child, his noisiness as a baby notwithstanding, and many recall him as a bit of a loner, which is perhaps unsurprising given the 11-year age gap between him and his nearest sibling. He must have in a sense felt like an only child, and his siblings may have seemed more like adults than contemporaries. He would attempt to tag along with his brother Derek's gang, but naturally the teenage Derek was not exactly overjoyed to have someone 12 years his junior cramping his style. In day-to-day life, it was normally his sister Daphne who paid him most attention.

It was Daphne who looked after him the most, too. In David Thomas's excellent book *Alan Sugar – The Amstrad Story*, there is an amusing tale about his first day at primary school. Sugar's sister Daphne took him along to school, and was shocked when he returned home at 11am. It seemed the youngster thought that morning play meant the school day had finished. Because he failed to pass the 11+ exam, Sugar was not eligible to enrol at a grammar school, and instead he went to the Joseph Priestley secondary. The school merged with another establishment soon after Alan enrolled, and the new institution was called Brooke House. There, he enjoyed a wonderfully varied educational experience. As he told David Thomas, 'I could still to this day build a brick wall if I had to. And I can still recite parts of Shakespeare. I can turn a lathe and read or draw a technical drawing. It was an amazing school.' He enjoyed studying science and engineering, and also took great pleasure from the classes in metalwork and technical drawing. Those who taught him back then were later to express surprise that he had made such a success of his life, as they found him in no way extraordinary during his childhood.

One of Sugar's earliest childhood memories is an unhappy one. As with a lot of people, some of his most vivid recollections of his earliest years revolve around a brush with illness that was to require medical attention. 'It's a bad memory,' he sighs. 'I was six and I was dumped in this cot in Hackney Hospital to have my adenoids out. I screamed and shouted, saying I should be in a proper bed, not a cot, 'cos I was six. I was still screaming when they put the mask over my face. Afterwards, my mother promised me I'd never have to go to hospital again. She conned me. A year later, I was in the same hospital, having my tonsils out.' In later years, Sugar has joked that he sometimes feels like a hypochondriac. Certainly, his appearances on *Friday Night with Jonathan Ross* always seem to contain a noteworthy level of medical chatter.

Sugar is proud of his Hackney heritage, and feels it has

very much shaped who he is as both a person and a businessman. 'I can't help the way I am,' he states firmly. Indeed, he wonders, why he would want to. 'My East End background might have made me a little rough round the edges, but that's not something I can do anything about. It was good training for reality; it kept me down to earth and taught me to quickly appraise situations and assess propositions.'

Those who have worked alongside Sugar, and also those who have been his rivals down the years, will attest to his sharp brain, and ability to analyse matters very wisely and efficiently. Even as his level of fortune and fame has rocketed skywards, he has always kept it real. 'I suppose the most telling thing about me is that I've been married to the same woman for 30 years,' he said, a few years ago. 'That's unusual for someone as rich and successful as me. But that's because I've kept the same values I had when I lived in a council house. I've come across people who went to the same cockney school as me. And I see them 30 years on, and they talk as if they went to Eton. And I know these are the same ratbags I sat next to at school in Hackney.'

Indeed, because there is no getting away from the reality that Sugar's childhood was by no means an entirely comfortable one, certainly not in financial terms. For instance, his parents refused to buy him a copy of the *Beano* comic, reasoning that he would throw it away once he had read it, and therefore it would be a waste of money. This atmosphere must have been an early jolt to his entrepreneurial spirit. As he put it himself, 'If you wanted pocket money you had to get it yourself.' Perhaps it is the way he rose from relatively humble beginnings to become such a successful and wealthy entrepreneur that makes him justifiably impatient with the excuses that some people throw up when explaining their own lack of success. 'I fought my way out of poverty and I remain convinced that others can do likewise too,' he has said.

However, amid the poverty that he fought his way out of, there were also some advantages, and ones that belong very much to a bygone era, perhaps never to be repeated. Sugar recalls this era, and its positive points, with a tangible wistfulness. 'We lived in the council blocks and we did all the good things. You could play in the streets, playgrounds, build bikes and carts. You can't roam around in these terrible times we live in now.' This East End spirit is one that many of those who hark from that area in that era will attest to, and Sugar mourns its loss in modern Britain. Not that Sugar is in anyway blind in his love of the area he came from, and the people who lived there back then. He feels he differs from some people that have come from his background. For instance, when asked whether he would drive further to go to a petrol station where the fuel was a few pennies cheaper, he insisted he would not. 'No, no, no, no. Definitely not. And nor would I work out which is the

cheapest mobile-phone operator and all that nonsense,'
he snapped.

He went on to explain that he felt people from his neck
of the woods – even the successful ones – often had this
tight-fistedness. Not him, though. 'Those kinds of people
wind me up terribly,' he roars. 'If they applied their
ingenuity to their businesses, they would be making far
more money than what they think they're saving. I
couldn't give a monkey's. If I had to go to a foreign-
exchange kiosk, I'd just walk up and say I want £200 in
dollars – I wouldn't even look at the rate of exchange.
But I've seen lots of other people from my sort of
background who have become successful but there's still
a stinginess about them, a stinginess that was needed
when they were at their grass roots but they can't get it
out of their system. I got it out of my system as soon as I
could afford things.'

He has also spoken out tetchily about how he is still
approached by people who claim they knew him in
Hackney 'back in the day', but who he doesn't remember.
As you can imagine, the straight-talking Sugar gives them
short shrift. 'You can see them coming from the corner of
your eye. He or she has been staring at you all night. No,
not plucking up courage, these people are the worst, they
are rude, they butt in, they have no common courtesy at
all. They say something like "You know my uncle in
Hackney." I say, "Oh, really?" "Yes, he says you know
him very well." Then they rattle off a name. I say, "No, I

don't know him, I've never heard of him." "Oh, but you do know him." "I don't know him, I'm sorry." "But you went to school with him, you must know him." Then I get a bit annoyed. Yes, sometimes I can be rude. I would probably say, "Well, I don't know him so clear off," or words to that effect.' This tendency would lead to a rather amusing episode concerning Rupert Murdoch later in his life.

Meanwhile, largely eschewing the after-school activities that were on offer at his various educational establishments, the young Alan Sugar preferred to head home and pursue some of his interests, pastimes and hobbies, which included photography and cooking. Both would soon be turned into more professional interests, and rather profitable ones at that. He began to make ginger beer at home, and sold it to his fellow pupils. This was done by feeding a ginger-beer plant each evening. He would then pour out the resulting drink and flog it to friends, undercutting the more expensive big-brand soft drinks such as Coke. He was following the example of his uncle, whom he describes as one of his earliest heroes. 'At the age of 17, my icon was my Uncle John, because he had a little corner shop in Victoria and was the only person I knew in business. As time goes by, you tend to overtake those people and look back in admiration. I've passed Uncle John, Harry the bloke who had the stall around the corner, Fred the chap who had the big electrical store, Bob the bloke who had the big warehouse and Frank the fellow big importer of electronics.'

It's not known whether Sugar believes in astrology, but those who do set store in that field would find much in him to back up their beliefs. Born under the Zodiac sign of Aries, which is suitably enough the Ram, he has gone on to display many of the associated traits: courage, initiative, stubbornness and straightforwardness are all said to be typical among Arians. Those born under this sign are also often said to be opinionated. Anyone who came up against him in *The Apprentice* boardroom in later years would go along with that. Some of these traits were apparent from an early age. He recalls himself as 'not a ruffian', but admits that, even as a child, with him there was 'always plenty of talk'. Could it be that some of that 'talk' was heard by his teachers when he was a schoolboy? Sugar attended the Brooke House School in Upper Clapton, Hackney. In a school report that was released to the media, one of the teachers who taught the young Alan Sugar, a Mr Robinson, gives an insight into what sort of pupil he was. He believes the teenage Sugar was 'an able boy' but he continues, 'He must take more care in the presentation of his work. A great improvement in his ability, but it is often misapplied. Alan is broadening his sphere of activities.' More interesting and revealing is the passage that covers Sugar's involvement in the sporting side of the curriculum. The teacher is full of praise for his pupil: 'A good year's work' from Sugar. He adds, 'Alan has represented the house in football and rugby. He has helped in the organisation of the teams. Well done, Alan.' Well done, indeed. And how fitting that a man who would go on to run a top-class English football club should have made such a great job in the organisation of football and rugby teams in his school days. If only he was similarly appreciated by the fans of that club.

Those school reports emerged in 1997, when Sugar returned to the school, which has since been renamed Hackney Community College, to launch its centre for construction, civil engineering and community education. It was an emotional and inspiring occasion for all. Sugar addressed more than 200 young people and talked to them about opportunities for starting their own businesses. A fun run also took place during the day, passing the old centres of the college, which housed the construction and engineering courses. Sugar, a charismatic speaker even before his *Apprentice* days, had the audience in the palm of his hand, as he told pupils that success requires 'hard work, focus and determination'. Naturally, the visit prompted headlines and Sugar's comments give an insight into how he looks back on his own childhood, and how he wants the best for the children of Hackney, where he took his first steps. He told reporters afterwards, 'I started out in business in Hackney as a kid and earned a living there as a kid, doing things that the youngsters of Hackney can do here today. I want to burn the spirit of entrepreneurship into them not to lecture them, but actually show them that business can be fun and that the rewards of hard work and common sense can be even more fun.'

After speaking to the reporters, Sugar also granted a then rare interview to BBC Radio 4's flagship *Today* programme. The sentiments he outlined there give an insight into how he sees the making of all entrepreneurs, including, of course, himself. 'You cannot make someone into an entrepreneur, just like you can't make someone a pop singer or an artist,' he said. 'It has to be in-built in you; it's a kind of a nose for things, a smell for things, and then an instinct to do it and a focus.' Interestingly, within years of his making these statements, reality television was indeed trying to 'make' pop stars and entrepreneurs right in front of our very eyes. However, Sugar's own slice of the reality television cake was about polishing, rather than making, businesspeople.

Let us return once more to his own childhood. Sugar insists that his love of business started at a very early age. 'I've been in business since I was a 12-year-old schoolkid, really,' he said. 'If there was an opportunity and a demand, I'd be there.' And, in common with all those who rise to the heights of entrepreneurial brilliance, Sugar found opportunities and demands wherever he looked, even back then. At the tender age of 11, he photographed other children and sold the resulting prints to their grandparents. As we've seen, he also made his own ginger beer and sold it to thirsty kids. Sugar went on to clean cars, a more traditional childhood enterprise but one that he went about with the trademark Sugar zeal. Later in life, rather than clean cars, he would be driven round in them, including an exclusive Rolls-Royce Phantom. Returning to the photographic sphere, he flogged repackaged black-and-white film and became something of a professional photographer. He would approach grandparents and offer to photograph their grandchildren for them. He would proudly present them with the finished black-and-white snaps, with 'Alan Sugar, photographer' neatly typed on the back. He had found a fertile ground for sales; offering to photograph grandchildren for half a crown, he found the grandparents' answer was always 'Yes, yes, yes.' They could never have enough pictures of their grandchildren.'

He was also a paperboy for a while, a job that allowed him to buy himself that copy of the *Beano* every week if that was what he wanted. By the time he reached the age of 12, the budding businessman would rise at the early hour of 6am to boil beetroot for the local greengrocer. 'It wasn't a case of deciding to do that: it was quite common for people who lived in my council block to have a Saturday job, a holiday job, a paper round or whatever,' he said, keen to play down the significance of the beetroot days. 'It was necessary – if you wanted your own pocket money you had to go and get it yourself.' Another job he took was at a local department store.

There, his natural brilliance as a salesman came to the fore. He was so good at selling footwear to the customers that he was offered the chance to promote himself from a Saturday job to a full-time job. It wasn't just his employers who noted his salesman's tack. Sugar also was described by his headmaster as someone who could sell anything to anyone. He himself had fallen for the charms of the Sugar sales pitch when his pupil asked him if he'd lend him the money to buy a printing machine, so he could produce a school magazine. 'With your cheek, I will,' replied his headmaster.

He also had a good grasp of mathematics, as many of those who go on to thrive in business are wont to have. He puts this down to a teacher called Mr Grant, whom he still remembers many decades on. 'I remember Mr Grant, the maths master, because, even though he gave up on me, I managed to pass my [GCE] O-level,' said the generous Sugar. 'He was a real eccentric. We used to call him Theta Grant because he made us laugh when he wrote the Greek letter theta on the blackboard. He was accident-prone. He'd come into school with his face smashed in or a broken arm. There were all sorts of rumours going round, but we never found out the cause of his injuries. When I discovered that the maths O-level syllabus involved something called calculus, which was supposed to be really difficult, I was fascinated. I've always enjoyed a challenge. I'm a quick learner and have a photographic memory. Within three or four weeks, I

13

became the whiz kid of calculus, which got me through the exam. Grant couldn't believe it.'

His shoe-selling days would be among the final times that Sugar ever worked for someone else. As he said, proudly, 'I haven't applied for a job since I was a teenager.' Although his success and riches have since brought him all manner of luxuries and pleasures, he insists that his original motivation to getting into business was far more down to earth and simple. 'When I first started out, I wasn't interested in making a million, I wasn't thinking about getting a knighthood,' he said. 'It was about getting some wheels. I wanted a car – and I wanted to be independent. I was also angry, and probably a bit arrogant. I was sick of putting money in other people's pockets when I knew I could earn more on my own.' This anger speaks of an internal frustration with life. Specifically, he feels that it came from seeing how his father had gone about his own working life. 'I had seen [him] work hard all his life, putting the family first and playing the safe game in order to take care of us.' Sugar felt that, in a highly important respect, he differed from his father, both in circumstances and makeup. 'I was at the point when I had no responsibilities – and I knew I didn't have his temperament – I would never be able to stay the course working for someone else.'

Therefore, his business ambition has been burning inside Sugar for as long as he can remember. He says he always felt he'd have his own business, and that at heart he has always been a salesman. 'I never wanted to be a rocket scientist or a football player,' he adds. He then turns again to the lessons he learned, and the conclusions he drew, from watching his father from a young age. Once more, we can see how he tried to differ from his father, though not to the extent of having anything less than total respect for the man. 'One of the things that drove me to be self-sufficient was looking at the way my father, a tailor, struggled to keep the family going. I thought, "I don't want that." He did a very good job of bringing up a family of four children in very tough times.'

There were tender moments among the tough times. For Sugar, his bar mitzvah would have been one of them. The words *bar mitzvah* translate as 'son on the commandment' and is the process Jewish boys go through at the age of 13. This is a great event in the life of a Jewish male, where he is called up to read from the Torah scroll. Often, the ceremony will be followed by an elaborate and at times wild celebration. For Sugar it was a more modest affair, which took place at a small synagogue in Upper Clapton Road. Nonetheless, this marked his coming of age. A few years later, he left school. 'It's generally said of me that I left school at 16,' he said. 'The precise truth is that I left school at 16 and three-quarters, having started A-levels at my London school.' He was the youngest in the family and the first to consider going on to higher education. 'My father was a tailor and the older children had left school and gone straight into the garment trade. So I suppose I was one of those council-house kids who had the makings of a great opportunity there, but the problem was that it just didn't suit me. I was simply the sort of person who wanted to get on with the rest of my life.'

However, Sugar did not move straight from school to becoming an energetic businessman. First he was to have a taste of office life working for someone else, but it was not to his liking and his experience of it was to ultimately make him even more determined to be the master of his own destiny.

CHAPTER TWO

YES MINISTER

After leaving school and taking his first steps into the big world, Sugar took a job as a civil service clerk statistician at the Ministry of Education and Science. This was a somewhat surprising choice for a man with Sugar's drive and imagination. It is perhaps not a surprise, then, that this is not an area of his life that Sugar is particularly fond of reliving. When one journalist asked him about it, he simply replied, 'It bores me talking about it again and again.' It is not surprising that Sugar is not full of enthusiasm for this part of his career. The civil service can be an oppressively procedure-driven industry, full of red tape. This has been excellently sent up in the BBC comedy *Yes Minister*, but it is unlikely that someone with Sugar's vision and entrepreneurial spirit would have seen the funny side of the civil service as he sat in dull and uninspiring surroundings.

So why did he end up there? Having been allowed to stay on at school longer than his father would have liked him to, and longer than some of his siblings had been kept in education, meant that Sugar felt he had to try to take on a more scholarly career. In any case, as he told David Thomas, 'Science – this was something I had always been interested in. Statistics, maths – I wasn't too bad at that. So I thought I'd go for it.' However, the work was almost cripplingly tedious, 'the most unbelievable bore going', he recalled. His tasks were so dull that one of the least objectionable parts of his job was calculating what percentage of children drank milk in the morning at school, which is hardly the sort of work that would appeal to Sugar. No wonder he shudders at the memory of the 'total agony' of waiting for the clock to run down each day, so he could get home!

Looking back on this time of his life, Sugar recalls how crestfallen he was when he realised quite how inappropriate his new job was to be. 'I was quite interested in science and engineering and naïvely took a job with the Ministry of Education and Science, expecting to be involved in interesting scientific projects,' he said. 'Imagine my disappointment when I was plonked into a boring office, pushing a load of paper around. This was not for me – though it was far from easy to tell my dad that I wanted out. The old man's priorities were security and a job for life. Yet here I was, a few months into the job and on my bike.'

It is almost extraordinary to think of Sugar in such surroundings. True, he has a fine mathematical mind and a great analytical ability. But Whitehall's civil service is for men who are the polar opposite of Sugar. To make his businesses work, he would relish the freedom, the creativity, the spark that secures that next avalanche of cash. Instead, here he was tied to a desk in a sterile atmosphere, with the nine-to-five mentality writ large in the very essence of the job description (although, to be fair, Sugar has always been a nine-to-five man who rarely takes his work home). His unsuitability for the role – or rather the role's unsuitability for him – can hardly be overstressed. His mother said that he didn't like it because it was 'a sitting-down job'. A nice succinct statement – one can see where he got his rough-and-ready wit of the *Apprentice* boardroom scenes.

Nonetheless, something really had to change before this young man was entirely broken by boredom. Many a man has taken an unsatisfying job, and somewhere along the line lost his spark and with it his ambition to leave, but Sugar was not about to get stuck in such a rut. To earn extra money, he took on a string of Saturday jobs, including one at a chemist's in Walthamstow. Another came at a clothes shop in London's West End. Here, he could perform tasks far more suited to his energetic, salesman nature. Soon, he was to leave his weekday job in the civil service to take a similar role at a British steel firm. Here, at least, his colleagues were more his type. There were banter and humour, two qualities that Sugar adored but that he had found entirely lacking in Whitehall. However, with their encouragement, he was soon to quit this job, too. He was ready to take his next step on the ladder to multimillionaire fortune. And, given his business success and the worldwide fame he found as the star of a television show, it proved to be an entirely prescient step.

Malcolm Cross was an East End television engineer. Sugar had known him for several years, after the pair originally met in the youth clubs of Stamford Hill. During his lunch breaks from his Saturday shift at the chemist's, Sugar would meet up with Cross and, as they ate their snacks, the pair discussed how they could break into business together. These were days of dreams and ambition. Soon, they had a plan to make a nice little earner together. They would buy cheap television sets that had seen better days; Cross would repair them and generally give them a spruce-up, then Sugar would use his skills and charms as a salesman to sell them on at a tidy profit.

The pair called their fledgling business venture 'Maurann', which was a combination of 'Maureen', the name of Cross's wife, and 'Ann', Sugar's girlfriend. Sugar even printed headed notepaper for Maurann, and they hired a room to store the televisions. It soon became something of a legend in the family. His brother Derek noticed an advertisement that said 'TV for sale' stuck to a local hot-drinks stall, and quickly realised where he recognised the phone number from: it was his mother's. As for Fay herself, she dubbed the repaired televisions 'old monstrosities', but that did not stop her from doing her part to help her beloved son in his venture. She would show customers up the stairs of the home to where the television was on display, and, if people came back to complain that the set they had bought was not working, she would simply hand over a refund.

However, there was a clever salesman's trick to this arrangement. As part of his sales pitch, Sugar would pretend that he had only one television set for sale, and that it was an unwanted gift to the Sugar family. He would lead punters into his bedroom, where only one set was on show, and then, as soon as that set was sold, he would replace it with a new one, to sell to the next visiting customers. It was a typically shrewd and effective sales tactic. The Maurann venture lasted no more than 12 months, but it was enough to fill the young Sugar with renewed confidence and energy.

Some of that confidence and energy enabled him to resign from the steel firm where he had been working. He remembers that his father was less than impressed by this latest career move. In less than a year, Sugar had gone through three different jobs, while his father had been in the same workplace for a decade and a half. Asked why he quit at that point, Sugar is typically honest and concise:

'What I was really after was wheels.' This was no small aim in those days, and, when asked what his earliest ever ambition was, he replied that it was to own his own car. 'A car was considered to be an absolute luxury,' he said. 'Rich people had cars – that's how you viewed it.' He couldn't afford one, but thanks to his spirited, entrepreneurial nature, he wasn't about to let that hold him back.

So it was that the man who would later own a Rolls-Royce Phantom got his hands on his first set of wheels – a company car as part of the package for his next job. He saw an advertisement from a London electrical firm for a salesman. The firm – Robuk Electrical – was looking to add to its army of salesmen across the country, and it seems that, on applying for the job, Sugar so impressed them that they gave him the task of selling across the capital. Sugar was on the sell and, thanks to the van that came as part of the job package, on the move. It was in this job that Sugar acquired an amazing knowledge of the capital city's many stores that sold electrical goods, a sector in which he would later make an absolute fortune. 'They gave me a minivan and, at the ripe old age of 17, I was flogging recorders to radio and TV dealers in north London,' he said, looking back. 'Within three months I was the top salesman. I quickly realised it paid to think big. I would talk my heart out to sell one tape recorder to a small shopkeeper. But, using the same energy talking to the chief buyer of Currys, I could get an order for 100 units. So I looked for bigger deals – and landed some great orders.'

Here, though, the arrangement didn't continue as expected for Sugar. He was initially delighted to be dealing with Currys. Up to then, he had been unable to do so because that store's managers had needed to contact head office before taking orders for tape recorders. Sugar saw this new arrangement as 'a licence to print money'. So, when he managed to persuade every Currys store in the capital to put orders in for Robuk tape recorders, he thought he was home and dry and that his commission rate would rocket. 'Instead of being rewarded, my commission rate was slashed,' he said. He had been told that, because the Currys deal was a bulk one, his commission was smaller than it would have been for a corresponding deal for the same number of independent stores. After a disagreement, Sugar resigned. Naturally, this latest parting of the ways didn't go down well at home. 'Third job over in nine months – the old man was tearing his hair out.'

Not that Sugar remains bitter about this episode – quite the opposite in fact. Like many of those who rise from mediocrity to become accomplished people, Sugar is not only able to shrug off past setbacks, but is also well versed at turning negatives into positives, at seeing how seemingly bad things in his past were actually wonderful things that set him on his way in life. 'Here's the payback,' he said, smiling. 'Had my ex-boss not been so ungrateful,

I might still be working for him today. I can't thank him enough. He made me determined to work for myself.' This is the sort of positive thinking and philosophical outlook that got Sir Alan Sugar where he is today. Modern self-help books preach just this sort of positive thinking, although, when he was starting out in business, such books scarcely existed. But then he didn't need them, because he naturally had most of what was contained within them, and what he didn't know he could pick up along the way. As he said himself, 'You can't learn to be an entrepreneur by reading a book. You can only find out by giving it a try. Don't worry if you make mistakes because that's how most people learn.'

He was soon in new employment. 'My next job was selling electrical goods to dealers,' said Sugar. His employers were R Henson Ltd, a wholesaler based in north London. Among the products he sold were walkie-talkies, car aerials, clock radios and car radios. He would show these products to retail customers and close the deal. 'I would talk my heart out to sell one tape recorder to a small shopkeeper,' said Sugar. Also, as part of his job he had to deliver the completed order and take the payment. Sugar says this job really opened his eyes to the world of business. Soon, frustration he felt with his new employers was to bubble over into another confrontation that led to his walking out.

'One day I pulled off a great deal on my own initiative,' remembered Sugar. 'Instead of congratulating me, my boss told me off for not earning enough money on the deal. That Friday I quit. Fourth job in a year.' The great deal he was referring to was a pile of records he sold on behalf of Henson's and returned with several hundreds pounds' profit. 'If Henson's had been clever at that stage, they would have made me a partner of the firm, and it might have been Henson's -cum-Amstrad by now,' he said, looking back. But, after his boss told him off for not earning more money on the deal, Sugar felt 'naffed'. So, off he went again in search of new work. However, although he felt naffed and walked out, he remained in contact with Henson's and even did business with them after he set up his own firm. The life lesson is clear: look at the bigger picture, don't be petty.

However, it was a nervous journey home for Sugar. 'I left the car and went home by bus, worrying what I was going to tell my dad,' he wrote. 'At that time he'd been in his job 23 years and was taking home £16 a week. I announced that I had walked out again and was going to start working for myself from Monday. My dad came out with this classic question: "Who's going to pay you on Friday?" "I'm going to pay myself," I replied.' As it turned out, he would make his first batch of money even more quickly than he had dreamed.

Gulu Lalvani was the founder and chairman of Binatone, the world's second-largest manufacturer of digital cordless phones. A tall, suave and attractive man, he was born in Karachi and raised in Bombay, and he

came to Britain as a student. He founded Binatone –
named after his sister Bina – in 1958 with his brothers
Katar and Partap to import radios from Hong Kong. He
has since gone on to become a businessman of some
repute, and one of Britain's richest Asians. Today,
Binatone International Limited is one of the largest
privately owned consumer-electronics companies in
Britain. It enjoys nearly 15 per cent market share in the
domestic-telephone sector here. Gulu also plays a major
role in Phuket's high-end property market, having
developed the Royal Phuket Marina on the east coast,
which features luxury apartments and villas. In 2008, he
invested a cool £1 billion in a Thai exhibition and
conference centre. But, back then, he was to become a
major player in the tale of Sugar's rise from Hackney to
the riches of Monaco.

During his short time with Henson's, Sugar used
regularly to collect goods from Binatone. He would turn
up to Binatone HQ in Finsbury Square, in London, and
wait his turn at the loading bay. Asked what is needed to
form your own successful business, Sugar once said,
'What you do need is sheer determination. Passion and
great personal belief. And a slice of good luck.' He was
about to be served a delicious slice of that good luck. As
he queued at Binatone's loading bay, he got talking to
Lalvani, who had already noted that Sugar had more
ambition and drive than most of those who queued at the
loading bay to collect goods.

Sugar also had an intelligent, enquiring way about him so he already had a firm grasp of how Henson's relationship with Binatone worked. Henson's received the Binatone products on credit, and sold them on for money, a perfectly normal way of doing business. 'I can do that,' thought Sugar. But he also believed he could earn four times his weekly salary of £20 if he went it alone. So he bought a minivan for somewhere between £50 and £80 (estimates vary in different accounts of this time), took out £8 in third-party insurance and approached Lalvani with an idea. He would resign from Henson's and give the Binatone man a postdated cheque. In return, Lalvani would give him goods to the value of that cheque. Lalvani was a little nervous, because he didn't want to fall out with Henson's, who might, reasonably, conclude that Sugar had been encouraged to compete with them. Sugar was quick to allay Lalvani's fears, telling him that he was going to quit with or without his help. As a compromise, Lalvani suggested that Sugar leave a two-week gap between resigning from Henson's and starting up his own firm. 'Deal,' said the 19-year-old Sugar.

Lalvani recalled that his protégé was a very quick learner. In an interview with the *Mail on Sunday*, he gave his impressions of the young Sugar: 'Alan used to drive a van for a customer of mine. He would come to the warehouse every day and buy electronics and sell them on.

'But his boss made a mistake: he let Alan see how much he was paying for the goods and where they came from and Alan knew the customers and how much they were paying. He came to me and asked for £500 credit. It wasn't difficult for me to say "yes". I could see he was energetic and hardworking. I told him he couldn't quit on Friday and start doing business on Monday – he had to wait.'

So, after two weeks with his feet up, Sugar returned to Binatone HQ and swapped the cheque for the goods. This cheque was postdated seven days hence. This meant that Sugar had just a week to shift all the goods, or he was in trouble. As it turned out, by the end of the first day of his new venture, Sugar had shifted the lot – a whole week's goods in one working day. He drove into the Binatone car park, and told an astounded Lalvani, 'Give me the cheque back. Here's the cash.' The following morning, he returned for more of the same. Recalling how he struck out alone in business, Sugar said, 'Your average punter sees no further than finding a job and working for someone else. Business is viewed as a risk – and people are frightened to take the risk in case they fail.' He had taken that risk, and, far from failing, he had exceeded even his own ambitious dreams. He must have been absolutely exhilarated. 'You will understand the buzz once you have done something on your own. In a funny way, the money takes second place.'

With his new business venture proving a huge success

from the start, Sugar could afford to be bullish and confident about his prospects. The world seemed indeed to be his oyster. However, his assurance was not shared by his father, Nathan, who was proving to be rather more cautious. His son's courage and entrepreneurial spirit soon caused more concern. The clash of personalities was to rear its head again when Sugar's minivan broke down. 'It was always in the bloody workshop,' said Sugar. 'We needed a more reliable vehicle because that was the lifeblood.' Too young to sign a hire-purchase agreement, he had to turn to his father for help in getting a new vehicle. However, his father was so concerned about Sugar's ability to keep up the payments on the agreement that he would sign only on the understanding that *he* buy the van and ask his son to pay *him* instead. 'It was the typical mentality of my father. He couldn't understand that I'd ever be able to pay the money back.'

He would of course be able to pay his father the money back. And, very quickly, he was earning more money than even he could have dreamed of.

CHAPTER THREE
MARRIAGE

For all his success and the millions he has made, Sugar has always been a family man at heart. He's firmly of the opinion that the only way to have a successful and happy life is to put your loved ones before your profits. He is a wonderfully loving husband and parent. At his side throughout his remarkable ascent to the top of the business world has been his beautiful wife Ann. After originally meeting her in 1968 through the youth club crowd of Stamford Hill, Sugar soon fell for the charms of young hairdresser Ann Simons. And she for his – though she admits that he was not like most of the other teenage boys she knew at the time. 'He was completely different from anybody else I had ever met,' she said. 'He wanted to work all the time. He wasn't like an ordinary 18-year-old boy.'

It seems her initial instincts were correct, for it seems

there has never been anything at all ordinary about Alan Sugar. Right back then, there were already those hallmarks of ambition, dedication and a superb work ethic that were to separate him from the pack.

However, as the pair's love developed, there was initially opposition to Sugar from his new girlfriend's family. They felt that he was from the wrong part of town, but, according to friends and colleagues at the time, this only made Sugar more determined to get his girl.

As we've seen, Gulu Lalvani, chairman of the electronics company Binatone, was one of Sugar's early backers and, in the *Mail on Sunday*, he gives an insight into the resistance Alan faced from Ann's family: '[A] customer of mine pulled me aside at my warehouse. He was very angry. He said, "See that young man? Tell him I don't want him to go out with my daughter." I told him that he had to tell him on his own. Johnny was a good customer. He wanted his daughter to marry a lawyer or a doctor. I told him Alan was a good customer and I couldn't say that kind of thing to him.'

So, despite these early difficulties, the couple's love blossomed, and they married at the Central Synagogue in Great Portland Street. An eyewitness remembered, 'The families put on a good show at the wedding – a clear sign that the Simonses were reconciled to Ann's choice. It was a very joyous occasion and both families seemed to get on just fine.'

Their first son, Simon, was born a year later. His father

was doing very well indeed by this time. At the age of 21, a lot of young people are still directionless, either still in education or in low-paid jobs, often spending their nights out at pubs or clubs, and it is hard to see how they will succeed. However, Sugar's life was far more dynamic at 21, and betraying more than a hint at the fortunes that were to come for this incredible businessman. Let 1 November 1968 become a key date in the history of British business, as it was on that day that Alan Sugar formed A.M.S. Trading Company (General Importers), and registered it as a limited company. Alan Sugar really *was* on his way.

As we have seen, to get there, he had overcome numerous obstacles. One of these involved a sharp lesson in the dangers that confront any business. He had been storing his stock in the family home in Marlands Road, east London, but there was no burglar alarm to protect it, and he had no insurance to cover it. With the benefit of hindsight, he admits that this was 'bloody stupid when you think about it', as one day a thief broke into the house and made off with all the stock. 'I wasn't completely flattened,' he said, but he quickly made sure that he got his own premises and took out the necessary precautions to protect his assets.

His premises were on St John Street in Islington. It was a slightly odd location. Across the road was the Sadler's Wells Opera House, and a mere stroll away were trendy eateries and posh antique shops. However, the new Sugar

HQ was in an area largely populated by other businesses, their storage buildings and workshops. It was on a busy main road, and generally the area lacked the charm that dominated nearby Islington, but he had a decent-sized premises that could safely store a substantial amount of stock. Next up, he needed an accountant, and he signed up with Guy Gordon, who not only managed his accounts, but also gave him plenty of general useful business advice.

For instance, the fact that A.M.S. Trading Company (General Importers) was a limited, rather than proper, company was down to Gordon's guidance. He told Sugar that this way of working would mean he limited his personal liabilities, and therefore mean his house and other personal assets would not be at risk if his business got into difficulties. Just as there are things to learn from the nature of the company, so there are from the name he chose: the A.M.S. part was clearly formed by Sugar's initials – Alan Michael Sugar. However, more revealing is that he chose the terms 'trading' and 'general importers', which suggests that at this stage his aspiration was not to make his own goods, but rather to import them and then sell them on at a profit. Exactly four years later, he would change the name of the company to A.M.S. Trading (Amstrad), although in reality he had been using that name for some time before he technically renamed it.

The name Amstrad is memorable, but Sugar says he simply took his initials, and welded them to the first syllable of 'trading'. 'It was more luck than judgement,' he insisted, adding that a lot of operations back then found their names in such a way. This was, after all, in the days before brand consultants appeared, delighted to charge extortionate fees in return for a catchy title to name your company.

An insight into how hard Sugar was working at this time in his career comes from a man who had his own premises near to Amstrad HQ, on Gray's Inn Road. Colin Lewin was an electrical trader who shared Sugar's physical build and much of his up-and-at-'em business style. They became friends and business contacts, swapping electrical products, advice and gossip. Sugar sometimes stopped by for a cup of tea near Lewin's premises. This happened only occasionally, purely because Sugar worked so hard. '[He] certainly put in a good six-day week,' recalled Lewin. These were tireless times indeed. As well as impressing Lewin with his work rate, Sugar was still very much impressing Lalvani of Binatone. One day, while loading up his van with electrical products that Binatone had imported from the Far East, Sugar learned that the company had taken delivery of a batch of radios that were faulty. He took the radios home and fixed them himself with the help of his wife, working hard overnight, having slogged hard all day. He was certainly a man full of energy and enthusiasm.

Lewin and Lalvani were not the only characters who

were impressed by the young Alan Sugar. Ronnie Marks was the owner of an audio store on London's Tottenham Court Road. Running from Oxford Street to Euston Road, this one-way street is a shopping heaven. Although at the north end it houses department and furniture stores, it is best known for its collection of cheap electrical stores. Laptop computers, stereos and DVD players are among the many goods available here at budget prices. The electrical consumer revolution of Tottenham Court Road was sparked in the 1960s, and Ronnie Marks was one of the first men to open a store there. He was also a wholesaler, and one day one of his counter staff told him that there was a 'new face out front' who was seeking some goods on credit.

The new face out front was Sugar, who found that Marks needed some convincing to give him any sort of credit deal. He had never met Sugar before, and was therefore unable to assess whether he could trust him. The irascible Sugar wouldn't back down and eventually a deal was struck. Marks would give him some goods on credit, but he would need to pay for them before he could return to collect a new batch of goods. True, this was a tight arrangement, but Sugar relished a challenge and selling was his forte, so it was not one that he feared. Like clockwork, at the end of each week he would return to the wholesalers with his money for the recent consignment, and ready to fill his vehicle with a brand-new batch of goods.

Once again, he had stepped up to the challenge and passed with flying colours. Within a matter of months, Marks was so impressed that he allowed Sugar more leeway, giving him four weeks to pay for each consignment. Even under this looser way of working, Sugar never let him down. Indeed, he was to regard Marks as a confidant. Like many who are successful early in their life, Sugar gained a lot of respect – but he also found he had to put up with a certain amount of condescension and patronising from some old-school business types. 'I can't stand doing business with him because he treats me like a little schoolboy,' Sugar confided in Marks, as they discussed a third party. 'He always calls me "son". I'd rather talk to his storeman.'

However, all the patronising people in the world couldn't hold Sugar back. His success and reputation soon snowballed. As he approached new wholesalers, he could refer any sceptical questions to those he was already working with, all of whom would give him a glowing recommendation.

Soon, though, Alan Sugar wanted to turn from a salesman into a manufacturer. The first major breakthrough that Amstrad had to this effect came in the hi-fi market. Sugar noted, back in the 1970s, that the dustcovers for turntables were very expensive. 'So I decided to find out how they were made,' he said. 'I'm a quick learner, when I want to be. I found out about injection moulding, how it was done, and got someone to make me a few thousand. Until then, I'd been buying stuff at £1 each, and hustling to sell it at £1.10. With the plastic tops, I became a producer, making something at four shillings [20p], which I sold for a quid. I'd risen above being just a buyer and seller.' He had invested £1,805 in the injection-moulding machine and he was quickly reaping the rewards.

However, the electrical stores that stocked turntables were also beginning to stock an entirely new kind of product – one that was to make Sugar an absolute fortune.

CHAPTER FOUR
COMPUTERS

As he sat in the Amstrad headquarters, computer engineer Mark Eric-Jones wondered who this charismatic late arrival to the meeting was. It seemed he had just stepped off a plane at Heathrow Airport and strolled into the meeting as if he owned the place. It was a lively meeting, but Eric-Jones noticed that, whenever this man spoke, everybody else would immediately fall silent and listen intently. Who was he? Mark Eric-Jones, meet Alan Sugar.

As the others at the meeting fell silent, Sugar announced that he wanted Amstrad to enter the home-computer trade. This was no vague dream of a rich man: he had a distinct vision as to how his company would pitch themselves in this growing market. Not only that, Sugar wanted to enter the market very quickly – within months. Warming to his theme, he eloquently outlined how he envisaged all this working. He wanted to launch a computer that was 'a real computer, not a pregnant calculator'. When it came to computers, for Sugar, size was everything. In the 21st century, computer manufacturers struggle to produce ever sleeker, thinner and more diminutive laptops. But, back in the 1980s, Sugar felt that bigger was definitely better.

He had first become interested in the computer market in 1982. Companies such as Commodore, Spectrum, Acorn and Oric were making a tidy profit selling home computers to a public who were fascinated by this new trend. At up to £300 a go, these computers were proving a very nice little earner. He wanted the model to have 'perceived value for money', and to gain that he wished to ape the sort of computers that the public normally saw only in airports and offices. Furthermore, this would be an all-in-one model. Those who purchased home computers back then normally had to buy a cassette recorder to plug into the computer, which was then itself plugged into the family television set. It was a complicated, cumbersome and rather ugly arrangement. The connections required were often baffling for a nontechnical generation, and, even if they managed to put the parts together successfully, they were rarely able to tune the television towards even a satisfactory sound and picture quality. Not only that, these computers were also bringing to the family home a whole new set of arguments. In addition to rows over which television show the family would watch of an evening came disputes about when the kids could play Pac-Man without interfering with their parents' favourite television show.

Sugar had noted this tendency and was determined that his product would be free of such problems. 'There were lots of rejects coming back because of mismatches on products,' he said of his rivals. Due to this confusion, he said, many computers were being not just returned to the shops, some of them were also being abandoned underneath customers' beds, never to be used. 'Our first computer was a very typical Amstrad concept,' he said. 'I decided that the Amstrad philosophy is an all-in-one piece, so we would present our product as complete with a keyboard, cassette mechanism and monitor.'

The other thing about the computer he dreamed of producing was of course its size. He quipped that his model would be far too big to be thrown under a bed, but of course there were other reasons as to why he thought big was beautiful. Putting himself in the place of a customer walking into his local Dixons store, Sugar said, 'He looks at this thing, with its whacking great big keyboard and a monitor, and he has visions of a girl at Gatwick Airport where he checks himself in for his holidays. And he thinks, "That's a real computer." . . . So that was my marketing concept: the old man, who has got to fork out a couple of hundred quid on kit because the kid is driving him mad for a computer, sees this thing that actually looks like a real computer.'

As we shall see, throughout the design process, Sugar's knack of understanding what makes the customer tick was vital in the creation of a winning product. At times, this would run counter to the more technical mindset of the team he assembled, but Sugar's commercial instincts would, quite rightly, prevail. Although Sugar's plans were very much focused on the 'man on the street', he also had a plan to give a nod to the business market. This was to prove to be the salvation of the entire project.

To get to the stage where Mark Eric-Jones would be sat in the Amstrad office wondering who Sugar was, the project had already taken many twists and turns. It was in August 1983 that Amstrad's Bob Watkins pitched up at the headquarters of Ambit International, carrying a large cardboard box. He opened the box and showed Ambit's Roland Perry a computer keyboard, with the Amstrad logo emblazoned on it. Watkins told Perry that Amstrad were attempting to design a new computer and that he wanted Perry to help them bring the project to completion. Sugar was a man in a hurry, not least because he had already been let down during his quest for the first Amstrad computer. Being new to this game, he had appointed a couple of engineers of his acquaintance to work on the software side of the project, while he and Watkins worked on the exterior design. However, the software designer suddenly left the project. When Watkins finally found the designer's home and gained entry, he found a rather chaotic scene with computer parts strewn everywhere. He eventually discovered that the disappeared designer had cashed a cheque in the north of England. Accordingly, a running joke for the project was born: that the team could always 'run off to the North' if things got too bad.

Therefore, time was of the essence and Sugar was actually demanding that the project be completed within five months. Perry first tracked down one of the designers involved in the project so far. He recalls being met by 'an oldish guy, bearded . . . and smoking a pipe' – not quite the youthful über-geek that Perry might have expected. As their conversation continued, it became obvious that the bearded pipe-smoker's teenage son had actually been doing most of the work on the project. No surprise, then, that Perry decided to build his team from scratch. For this he turned to Britain's then equivalent of the Silicon Valley – which was Cambridge University. There he met with two sets of designers. One of these teams was unsettled by the fact that Perry couldn't tell them – due to Sugar's request for secrecy – who the client was. However, the second team he met were far more enthusiastic.

All seemed to be going well as Perry met the team, but, when the team were asked how long it would take them to complete the job, their answer was 'about eight months', which was considerably longer than the timeframe Sugar had demanded. Perry and the team talked on, moving to a local pub for a drink and a bite to eat. So it was that the King's Arms pub in Dorking was the venue for the discussions that would make Sugar's vision come true and in the timeframe he had in mind. Compromises were reached, technical details tweaked and a deal was thrashed out. A few days later, the team were invited to Amstrad headquarters, where, as we've seen, Mark Eric-Jones had discovered the identity of his client. He was quickly impressed by Sugar. 'He was the exact opposite of some people who just muddle around,' recalls Eric-Jones. 'He had this immense clarity in his ideas and in what he was trying to achieve.' It was game on.

This was a lean and mean game, too. As David Thomas explains in *Alan Sugar – The Amstrad Story*, the resources and timeframe for the project dwarfed those offered elsewhere in the industry. 'When IBM designed its first personal computer, admittedly a more complex machine, it gave 26 in-house engineers, supported by 100 manufacturing technicians and an array of sub-contractors, a year to complete the project – and this went down as a miracle of speed in the annals of the world's biggest computer company.'

Sugar, meanwhile, was giving six engineers less than five months to design Amstrad's first computer. As Eric-Jones put it, 'It was sufficiently close to impossible to do in that timescale that it was a very exciting challenge.' A statement oozing with ambition and humour – and he'd need plenty of both to pull off the task. An abundance of frozen pizzas helped too, he recalls.

Amstrad's culture did clash with that of the designers on occasion. Due to security issues, the Amstrad office worked very set hours of 9am to 5.15pm. So it was that, ten minutes before closing time each day, a security guard would give the staff notice to quit the building and the whole team – including Sugar himself – would exit. The Ambit team were used to more relaxed working hours, and so communication was tricky as the two teams were both working consecutively for only a few hours each day. But this problem was lessened because Amstrad were actually quite happy to leave Ambit to get on with it for most of the time. They did, though, get regular demonstrations and these would see Sugar's customer-focused mindset clash with the Ambit technical mentality. Sugar's perspective tended to win the day.

After numerous ups and downs, more than a few dramas and plenty of the aforementioned pizzas, the Ambit team hit its deadlines and the first Amstrad home computer was completed and launched in April 1984. The imaginative launch took place at a grand Westminster hall and the new machine was reviewed enthusiastically by the trade press. Guy Kewney of *Personal Computer World* gave it a thorough testing and liked what he found. 'The Amstrad is a powerful, fast machine, with plenty of memory, easy to program, and packaged in a way that means it will comfortably outsell the Acorn Electron, and give the Commodore 64 and Sinclair Spectrum a hard run for their money. I expect some 200,000 systems to be sold by the end of the year.'

Although the home-computer market was to peak soon after the launch, the fact that Sugar had given a nod to the business market in the design of his model and the fact that he marketed the computer elsewhere in Europe meant that he sold out and made a nice profit.

The marketing in Europe had been handled brilliantly by Sugar's contacts overseas. For instance, in France, Marion Vannier promoted it as 'The Anti-Crisis Home Computer'. Again, the strength of Sugar's 'tower concept' was to the fore here. She was a woman very in tune with Sugar's ethos. She once said of Amstrad's French operation that 'We transform elitist products into mass products. We seed new markets.'

Meanwhile, Jose Luis Dominguez in Spain was also enthusiastically promoting the Amstrad model. Soon, the overseas sales were getting higher and higher: from £10 million in 1983/84 to £174.9 million in 1985/86.

It was at this point that Sugar planned to enter the word-processor market. During a flight to Hong Kong, he produced a rough sketch of the model he had in mind. It took his liking for the 'all-in-one' concept to a new level by including the printer in the one-piece model. He codenamed the project 'Joyce' after his secretary of the time. Again, Sugar was looking for a slick and speedy operation to bring his dream to fruition. He also wanted it to be very competitive in value. This would be a professional-standard business computer that would sell for the user-friendly price of less than £400. Just five years earlier, such machines would have sold for up to £10,000. Once more, Sugar was bringing the computer to the budget of the people. His attention to detail in this regard paid dividends. When he sat down to read the instruction manual that the engineers had produced, he was horrified. It was full of the most impenetrable jargon imaginable. 'They all thought they were going to get the Nobel Prize,' he snapped, showing the neat line in sarcasm that was to become his trademark on *The Apprentice*. 'From an engineering point of view, the book was fantastic. It had cross references for every single detail of the Z80 processor. But that doesn't tell somebody how to write a quick letter about selling a lawnmower.'

The model – and an improved manual – completed, it was time for the launch, which took place in August 1985 in a London conference centre. Three actresses were hired to play the part of secretaries: one who would use only hugely expensive word processors, one who would use a typewriter and one who would use the affordable Amstrad word processor. Sugar told the launch bash that his model would 'blow the lid off the personal-computer and word-processing market'. He was bringing the word processor into the range of the little guy, he said, and, despite its cheap price, it included 'features that will make the transatlantic names wince'.

The trade press were also impressed, and the word processor received some glowing reviews. *Which*

Computer magazine said it was 'truly amazing for a computer in this price range'; *Popular Computing* added that 'nothing else comes close'; while *Personal Computer World* praised its 'spectacular value for money'. *Electrical Trade and Retailer* was similarly taken with the model, and its conclusion must have been particularly welcome to Sugar: it praised it as 'a grown-up computer that does something people want, packed and sold in a way that they can easily understand, at a price they'll accept'. This positive publicity was due in part to the charm offensive that the computer division of Amstrad – called Amsoft – had undertaken with the gentlemen (they were rarely women in computer magazines) of the press. Although schmoozing the press was not a part of business that Sugar enjoyed, he allowed Amsoft to do as they saw fit.

Other developments in the computer business that Sugar was not too keen on, but that he nonetheless went along with, included the launch of an Amstrad Users' Club. Everyone who bought the word processor would have found inside the box a leaflet with a smiley photograph of Alan Sugar on it. 'Now you have bought the computer, why don't you join the club?' read the text. All these new features were helping to make Amstrad bigger and bigger players within the computer market, and Sugar was loving it. He said of this latest model, 'The pundits thought we were bloody mad again . . . They looked at us as the poor relation who needed to go to the mental asylum.' But, he boasted, he had had the last laugh as he brought 'computing to the people who never even thought they would use a computer'.

The advertisements promoting the machines were impressive. Featuring old typewriters being thrown into a scrapyard, they boasted of the brilliance of the Amstrad Word Processor, concluding, 'It's more than a word processor for less than most typewriters.'

Meanwhile, Sugar had personally visited trade outlet heads to sell them on the charms of the model. He did it well: Dixons took an initial order for 20,000 models after meeting Sugar. This was a good move, because it took off wonderfully. 'It was one of the great phenomenal takeoffs in my experience,' recalls the Dixons chairman. He added that it was a 'bombshell' to him how well it sold. Not that he had doubted it had potential. 'The dream of a business of ours was that computers should cease to be exclusive, magic products,' he said. 'They would become consumer electronics. That was the great breakthrough. That was the measure of Alan's genius.'

Another measure of his genius quickly followed: a trebling of Amstrad profits from £9.5m to £27.5m. In trebling his profits, Sugar had shown his opponents in the computer market who was boss. One of those opponents would soon come knocking on Sugar's door with a very interesting proposal.

While in Hong Kong in 1986, Sugar was called to an

unexpected meeting with the managing director and chairman of Dixons. They told him that, in short, Sir Clive Sinclair was looking for somebody to take the Sinclair computer operation off his hands. Clive Marles Sinclair was born on 30 July 1940, and had enjoyed a comfortable childhood living near posh Richmond in Surrey, just west of London. Even as a child, he was an inventor, and his bedroom was always chock-full of wires and electrical equipment. Indeed, at a young age he had designed a new type of submarine. His first job was an editorial assistant for a magazine called *Practical Wireless*. In 1972, he invented the first true pocket calculator, and he then went on to create the Sinclair Spectrum, which was a popular home computer during the 1980s.

However, by the end of 1985, Sinclair Research (the company behind his computers) was not making financial sense. He was having to sell his computers to Dixons at a dramatically knock-down price just in order to keep his business viable. However, the company was still a strong player in the computer industry so Sugar was quickly tempted by the possibility of taking over the operation, a deal that at a stroke would make him the biggest player in games computers. He was also convinced that his famously efficient and lean business ways would no doubt see him make the operation more efficient and profitable. So it was that Sugar and Sinclair met for lunch in Liverpool Street, London, to discuss the deal. This was indeed a power lunch, with two of Britain's leading businessman at the table. Sugar felt very much on the rise, while Sinclair was perceived as being on the way down. As the *Guardian* had recently commented: '[1985] was the year that Mrs Thatcher's golden hopes for Britain's high-tech future – Sinclair, Acorn and Apricot – came a cropper. And the year that former replacement car aerial salesman and budget hi-fi king Alan Sugar skilfully steered his company Amstrad to become the driving force of the UK micro scene.'

Sinclair was as posh and geeky as Sugar was brash and outspoken, but the struggling inventor liked his opposite number. 'I found Alan Sugar a delightful man to deal with,' he said. 'He tended to say this is the deal. He never tried to improve his position or deviate from what he said he would do. He was very straightforward and clear-headed. He was very pleasant company, enjoyable to meet – a witty man.'

However, the amount of money that Sinclair expected to receive in the deal was far more than Sugar envisaged. He left the meeting convinced that the deal would never go ahead.

But Sinclair was keen to close a deal and so, at Eastertime, the prospect of a deal appeared to be back on. At a meeting in the City, Sugar offered £5 million for the operation and was prepared to part with £11 million for the stock inventory. He was about to go on holiday – his ticket for the Concorde flight to Florida was in his briefcase – so Sugar summed up in particularly concise style. 'That's the deal I'm offering, but I haven't much time. So if you're interested, fine. If not, it's nice to have met you and I'll say goodbye.'

Those representing Sinclair attempted to negotiate a higher figure from Sugar. At one point they even asked him to leave the room, and then asked him to increase his basic offer to £10 million. Sugar refused, and Sinclair backed down to accept the original offer. Sugar left the meeting, dashed to the airport and settled into his seat on Concorde. It must have felt good.

Over the next week, the final details were thrashed out and, at times, it looked as if the deal might stall after all. Sugar was tough and steadfast throughout, and reflected afterwards that the Sinclair people thought they were dealing with 'a boy who had just got bar-mitzvahed . . . someone with too much money and didn't know what I was doing.'

However, Sugar got his way and the deal was sealed. He returned to England and just 48 hours later was at the joint press conference to announce the deal. He remembers that the assembled press encouraged him to goad Sinclair about the deal. But, ever the gentleman, Sugar resisted the bait. 'The deal is good for both of us,' Sugar told the hacks. 'Sinclair is good at research and this gives them money to press on with it. We are good at marketing and this gives us another wonderful product to sell.'

Clive Sinclair echoed the sentiment that each side of the deal would play to its strengths. 'We pioneered the market. Now we've handed it over to the people who are experts in international marketing. It gets us out of a business we were not doing very well in, and allows us to continue in interests we do well in. We chose the Amstrad deal because it was a better deal. We sold off the traditional business.'

The Amstrad press release announcing the deal read: 'Amstrad Consumer Electronics PLC today announced that it has purchased from Sinclair Research Ltd the worldwide rights to sell and manufacture all existing and future Sinclair computers and computer products, together with the Sinclair brand name and those intellectual property rights where they relate to computers and computer-related products.' The Sinclair announcement used the same wording.

Naturally, the deal made huge news around the world. 'Sinclair Research Sold' ran the headline in the *New York Times*. The *International Herald Tribune* called the deal the 'most widely followed $7 million corporate transaction in British history'. 'Sinclair forced to sell patents to pay debts,' echoed *The Times* in London. The *Guardian* ran with 'Sinclair 20 million pound debts force sale to rival: Amstrad buys out pioneer home computer firm' and Canada's *Globe and Mail* went with 'Sinclair Sells Out to Rival Amstrad'. The *Economist* described Sugar's deal as a 'neat catch'. The report began: 'What goes up must come down, and British entrepreneur Sir Clive Sinclair this week did – into the arms of rival Mr Alan Sugar, founder and boss of Amstrad Consumer Electronics.' The *Financial Times* said that the deal was so logical 'it could have been conceived by an electronic brain'. Meanwhile, *Campaign* magazine said, 'Only the foolish would attempt to dispute Alan Sugar's claim that he has a natural talent for business, just as others have for music.' However, even this praise would probably not have made Sugar as happy as the *Daily Telegraph* comment that 'The man who knew what the technology could do has lost to the man who knew what the customer wanted.'

As expected, Sugar immediately made sure the Sinclair part of his empire was run in a more streamlined manner. He took the manufacturing overseas, having quipped at the press conference that 'We would like to manufacture in the United Kingdom, but we're a computer company, not a benevolent society.' Production was moved to the Far East as Sugar injected some lean, wise Amstrad thinking into the Sinclair operation. By happy coincidence, Amstrad had recently appointed a designer with Sinclair experience. Soon, Sugar was shifting tens of millions of Sinclair computers each year.

He was also becoming an increasing media star. As Amstrad rose and rose, he was widely profiled and even appeared on the BBC's flagship chat show *Wogan*. Indeed, his triumphant year in 1986 saw him awarded gongs in newspaper round-ups. David Kelly wrote in the *Guardian*, 'If 1985 was Atari's year, then last year belongs to Amstrad. After triumphant sales of its PCW home workstation during Christmas 85, Amstrad surprised everyone buying up Sinclair with the change from its back pocket.'

Not that all the coverage was so complimentary. Gareth Powell, of the *Sydney Morning Herald*, wrote, 'Sugar has spice, but he is not quite nice. At least this is the attitude of the computer journalists in Britain.' However, on examining the case of Sugar, Powell concluded that much of the criticism of him seemed unfair. 'In the past few weeks,' he wrote, 'I have been told by journalists that Sugar is a "business thug", whatever that may mean, and that he is never seen in public without two bodyguards.' However, when Powell encountered Sugar at a public press conference, he said no bodyguards were to be seen and that numerous enquiries failed to produce any proof that Sugar employed bodyguards at all. Powell concluded that jealousy and snobbery were largely to blame, together with a very English suspicion towards success.

Powell has a point on both envy and snobbery. In contrast to, say, America, success seems to be something that is rarely celebrated in Britain. This is a country where spectacular failures such as ski-flop Eddie the Eagle Edwards are treated as heroes, but golfing winners such as Nick Faldo are often treated with disdain; a country that produced the poet Rudyard Kipling, who encouraged readers to treat triumph and disaster as 'impostors' to be reacted to in exactly the same way; a country whose most stirring battle poem is, as George Orwell pointed out, 'about a brigade of cavalry which charged in the wrong direction'. Meanwhile, as the *Daily Telegraph* pointed out in 1987, 'Yet despite . . . the rise of a new species of working-class entrepreneurs like Alan Sugar, most of Britain's largest fortunes remain in the hands of the landed aristocracy.'

But *Fortune* magazine had just dubbed Sugar one of Europe's key 'new entrepreneurs', *The Times* called him one of the men 'who hold the aces' and the *New York Times* had just described him as 'Europe's most successful entrepreneur of the 1980s', and this three years before the decade ended. *Fortune*'s profile of him had been gushing. 'Sugar, who started out hawking car antennas at 16, relishes price wars. He shook up the British stereo and PC markets with cut-rate products that are technologically conventional but expensive looking. In the year ended June 30, Amstrad's sales more than doubled, to $426 million. "We produce what the mass market wants," declares Sugar, "not a boffin's ego trip."'

Speaking of ego trips, Sugar never entered business for public acclaim or out of any need for acceptance, so he may have taken all this praise with a pinch of salt. Nonetheless, it was a good reflection of his growing stature that so many column inches were being devoted to him. This media attention would stand him in good stead, for in the next two decades he would become even more famous.

Away from the business, Sugar is a keen tennis player. He particularly got into this game during the 1980s, and the combative zeal that marked all his business dealings was just as apparent on the tennis court. By the end of the decade, he had become a very fine tennis player, so much so that he organised a pro-celebrity tennis evening at the Royal Albert Hall. It was June 1989 and the Wimbledon tennis tournament was just around the corner, and, as ever at this time of year, tennis fever was sweeping the nation. The event, sponsored by Amstrad, was held in the prestigious Royal Albert Hall in London. Among the television personalities to compete were *Minder* star Dennis Waterman, comedian Jimmy Tarbuck and chat-show legend Terry Wogan. Footballer Bobby Moore also turned up.

In the semifinal of the tournament, it was very much a battle of the business giants when Sugar was drawn against Virgin tycoon Richard Branson. Sugar was not without support as he took on Branson. Alongside him was Indian tennis legend Vijay Amritraj, and all round the plush venue were supporters. There were banners and chants offering him their support. 'Come on, Alan!' and similar chants, filled the air. Sugar and Amritraj beat Branson and his partner, and marched on to win the final. He had really developed a great technique for the game, having practised on holiday in the Catskill Mountains and in Florida, and also while at home at weekends. However, the real winner was the Muscular Dystrophy Group, for which the evening raised a wonderful £170,000.

Having incorporated the computer operation of rivals Spectrum into the Amstrad fold, it was now time for Amstrad to turn its gaze to another computer giant. This time, though, rather than making it part of the family, Amstrad would take on its rivals head on. With more than 388,000 employees worldwide, IBM is a technology giant and is widely considered to be the world's largest computer company. Back in the mid-1980s, IBM were shifting in excess of 2 million computers every year. It was around this time that Amstrad decided to build its own IBM-compatible model. This was a response to pressure from its overseas contacts. When Sugar badgered them to sell more of his word processors, they would reply, 'No, no, no, we can't sell that. We want an IBM-compatible.'

So, in the second half of 1985, the project to build the first IBM-compatible Amstrad machine was launched. This time, the codename for the project was Airo, which stood for Amstrad's IBM Rip-Off. This was merely a joke, though, because Amstrad was making sure that its new machine would not copy an IBM model. Once experts saw the finished product, they were impressed. Paul

Bailey of Digital Research hailed it as 'revolutionary'. *The Times* called it 'a personal computer coup for Amstrad'; the *Economist* described Amstrad at this point as 'A British David' (as opposed to Goliath) in the computer world. A week on from the launch, *The Times* reported again on the PC1512, rounding up the critical response: 'First reports from those few computer reviewers who have been able to lay their hands on a new Amstrad computer are encouraging – more impressed than expected seems to be the most popular view.' The *Guardian* described the model as 'a fast 8086 machine that costs a fraction of its IBM competitor'. The newspaper added, 'While Amstrad is famous for cost cutting, the company has not skimped on the PC1512's performance.' *Personal Computer World* was little short of gushing in its praise: 'It goes faster than the IBM, it's smaller, has better onscreen colours, and includes functions which have to be added (and paid for) separately on normal IBM-style machines.' The following year, *Which?* magazine named the PC1512 its 'best buy'.

As for Sugar, he saw it as a multipurpose machine. 'I see it as a real home computer where father can bring work home from the office on a floppy disk, put it in his machine and work on it on his own desk, before taking it back with him into his office in the morning,' he said. 'At the same time, "Sonny Jim" can use it to play Space Invaders if he wants.' He made this statement at the grand launch of the model, when nearly 1,000 hacks turned up to the Queen Elizabeth Conference Centre in London to be met by a huge pair of red lips on a giant screen. Those lips explained what the many benefits of the PC1512 were. The eight differing models that formed the PC1512 range were then unveiled. A reported £3.5 million was spent on advertising the model, and the accompanying television advertisement cheekily said, 'Compatible with you know who. Priced as only we know how.'

A tempting prospect. Too tempting, at first, it turned out. In the opening months of sales, customers found it increasingly hard to get their hands on a PC1512 model because initial demand had far outstripped Amstrad's projections. Obviously, this was a nice problem for Amstrad to have and contributed to a 50 per cent increase in the company's share price. A more serious problem was the rumours that the models overheated. Although there was some truth to these rumours, there was also evidence that a dirty-tricks campaign was under way against Amstrad's new computer. Sugar was incensed by this, and said it was worse than anything he had experienced in previous years. 'When I was competing against 40 other small-time dealers [in the hi-fi market], who'd kill their grandmothers in order to beat me to a deal . . . these dirty tricks and lies were never thrown at us.'

To counter the overheating rumours – rumours Sugar denied – he agreed to build a fan into the PC1512. This did not constitute an admission on his part that a fan was needed. It was more about reacting to customer concerns. He joked that, if customers wanted bright-pink spots on the computers, he would react the same way.

However, the rumours had proved damaging and Sugar's fury and disgust at the dirty tricks is justified. In October 1986, it was reported that chemicals company ICI had opted not to buy the PC1512 for use in its offices, due to concerns about overheating and performance. However, the truth was that ICI had made no such decision and were still involved in tests. To clear the matter up, ICI wrote an open letter to Amstrad. It read, 'During the trials no problems were experienced with overheating when the Amstrad PC was connected to a token ring network. The Amstrad PC1512 has now been approved for purchase by ICI operating units.' Nonetheless, damage had been done to the model's reputation by the regular whispers and reports.

Not that Amstrad has ever been backwards in coming forwards, and after a report in the BBC staff magazine *Ariel*, which threw doubt on the safety of the PC1512, Sugar put his men into action. Nick Hewer, of Michael Joyce Associates Public Relations, and the man who would later stand alongside Sugar on *The Apprentice*, spoke of how he responded to the growing controversy. 'When the safety of the PC1512 was being questioned by the BBC in its magazine *Ariel*, the writ came so fast their feet tingled. Harmful publicity was difficult for us to deal with. We waited for the biggest one to get it wrong – and they apologised within 24 hours. We couldn't let it carry on.'

At the launch of the model, Sugar had proudly boasted that he expected to sell 300,000 models by the end of the year, and in the first full year of sales he expected to shift 800,000. More than 50 per cent of these sales, he predicted, would come from outside Britain. These optimistic projections, combined with the whizzing early sales, led to disappointment when the projections were not ultimately reached. There was a dramatic decline in Amstrad's share price in 1987. In June of that year, almost £300 million was knocked off the company's market value. Relations between the City and Amstrad were often not great. One City analyst accused Sugar of being a Trappist monk, and then –even more bizarrely – compared him to the Islamic prophet Mohammed, a rather strange combination of characters to compare any man to. Sugar was succinct as ever: 'There should be some professional exam for these analysts. Most of the time they talk through their backsides.' If such an exam were to include a mathematics question, then the analysts could have feasted their eyes on the following set of statistics. In the financial year 1986/97, Amstrad's profits were up 80 per cent at £135.7 million. Sales were up 68 per cent at £511.8 million.

No wonder Sugar was in bullish mode as he wrote the chairman's statement for the year. 'The Amstrad effect of course rocked the boat,' he said of the computer world. 'The resultant factor being critical comments of the product with which I am sure all and sundry are familiar. I think Pythagoras and Columbus had the same problem when they announced the world was round.'

It was around this time that Sugar gave his speech to City University mentioned in this book's Preface. There he had outlined the lean and mean nature of Amstrad. Ironically, this speech almost served as a coda to that era. For Sugar's company was about to go through a number of significant changes. 'There is a temptation to follow the experience of other companies which have risen, like Amstrad, to great heights,' wrote Sugar in the chairman's statement of 1987/88. He described these companies as wandering 'like a lost lamb with a shopping basket'. Amstrad, he decreed, would be different. It would react to its success by creating overseas subsidiaries. Out would go the 'middle man's margin', in would come more control over its 'destiny'. Soon, the company had formed subsidiaries in many nations including Australia, Belgium, Italy, the Netherlands, Spain, the United States and the old West Germany.

Another significant change came about not as a result of Sugar's forward thinking, but as a consequence of what many regarded as the backward thinking of the European Community, which began to levy huge duties on goods imported from Japan. This was fine for the giant electrical firms such as Philips (who were supporters of this trend) but not good news for Amstrad, who relied on the cheaper prices of Far East manufacturing. However, his opposition was not just a matter of self-interest. The customer too would pay, because it would be harder for any company to offer them discount prices. And where, some wondered, would the next Amstrad come from if these restrictions continued? It was all very well for the giant multinationals who could afford to make components themselves. A fledgling firm would find it a much more uphill task.

As Sugar explained, this new legislation may have been passed to try to protect industry in Europe, but it was about to have the opposite effect. 'The EC is being too protectionist. It's going to hold back people like myself in future. It's very fashionable in the EC for big companies to sit back and complain about the rest of the world.' No wonder he was so frustrated with what he called 'the gnomes of Brussels'. However, he did visit the Trade and Industry Secretary Lord Young, to let his opposition be known. He also told a BBC programme, 'If [Margaret Thatcher] knew what was going on she would do her nut.' As the new legislation tightened its hold on his businesses, he visited the gnomes of Brussels to plead his case. He returned with the conclusion that they were 'a total sham'. Not that Sugar felt the same about European businessmen. Quite the opposite, in fact. 'The European businessman is the best in the world,' he has said. 'They are in a class so much above the Americans and Japanese it's untrue.'

Tough times for Amstrad and other companies like it. However, at least Sugar's multinational sales drive and new subsidiaries system was paying dividends. Soon, sales in Britain constituted only half of the sales the company was enjoying. The rest was made up by overseas sales, including 19.4 per cent in France, 17.3 per cent in Spain and 5.4 per cent in North and South America. Sugar's reputation was on the rise. As a result, he was having an increasing number of the aforementioned approaches from people who claimed they were old friends of his from Hackney, but whom he could not recall ever knowing. It's a peril that befalls many who are rich and well known. 'The school I went to in Hackney must have had 250 million boys in it, because everybody that phones claims to know me, or went to school with me, or knows a brother who's got an uncle who knows an aunt who knows me.' As a result, Sugar took to asking his secretary to screen such calls, politely but firmly.

This was a sensible course of action, but it led to one memorable and – in retrospect at least – amusing episode. In May 1988, Sugar's secretary told him that a Mr Rupert Murdoch was on the line. Without even looking up, Sugar – who readily admits that he is terrible at remembering names – replied, 'Never heard of him. Tell him to piss off, clear off . . . I bet he thinks he went to my school.' He added that, unless this Rupert Murdoch would say what he was calling about, he wouldn't take the call.

His secretary returned with the news that 'Mr Murdoch doesn't normally tell people what his business is before speaking to them himself,' and had consequently rung off.

'But who is he?' asked Sugar.

His secretary replied, 'He owns the *Sun*, *The Times*, the *Sunday Times*, the *News of the World* and *Today* newspapers.'

Sugar was horrified at his error. 'Oh my God,' he said. 'Quick, get him back on the line.'

Not that this episode did anything to harm Sugar's standing with Murdoch, who has since described him as 'probably Britain's greatest entrepreneur'.

Sugar was delighted by this compliment when he was informed of it during a newspaper interview. 'He said that? I really admire Rupert Murdoch. When he wanted to own a TV station in America, the law was you can't unless you're an American. So, instead of giving up, he became an American. But he's laughing up his sleeve, because he still thinks he's an Australian! That's the kind of logic I like.' He went on to speak of not just Murdoch, but other businessmen he admired. 'He's a good bloke. And, well, yeah, I suppose I have to admire Richard Branson. Apart from all that self-promotion stuff, he's got a bloody good business with that airline. His cola drinks apparently aren't doing too well, but at least he has a go. Yeah, I like that. Good on him.'

For the record, he has since spoken fondly of other businesspeople, including Microsoft founder Bill Gates. 'You can only admire him for his vision that software was going to drive the computer industry,' he said with a smile. 'When we were the kingpins of the computer business in the UK and Europe, he came to my home and sat there discussing business. I'm not saying that we're bosom buddies and that we call each other up all the time, but if you mentioned my name I'm sure that he would know me.'

Another company that knew of Sugar was closer to home. Formed in 1975, Viglen provides IT products and services, including storage systems, servers, workstations and data/voice communications equipment and services to the education and public sectors. In 1994, Amstrad acquired Viglen and three years later it was listed as a public company. Sugar described the Viglen acquisition as 'the start of a new direction' for Amstrad. 'We are delighted that Viglen and its senior management team are joining the Amstrad group. We have looked carefully at many acquisition opportunities and consider that Viglen provides an exciting new dimension to Amstrad's existing businesses,' he said.

As for Viglen, they echoed Sugar's glee. Vig Boyd, the company's managing director, said that he had been looking forward to becoming a part of the Amstrad group. 'We look forward to becoming a wholly owned, but nevertheless independent, subsidiary of one of the largest British electronics companies,' he said. 'Viglen will continue to develop, manufacture and directly sell high-quality, innovative PCs.'

To this day, relations are fantastic. Viewers of *The Apprentice* would recognise the Viglen headquarters in St Albans as the location for the infamous interviews round that precedes the grand final. Indeed, Bordan Tkachuk, the CEO of Viglen, is one of the men who give the candidates the notoriously tough grilling in that round.

With his reputation on the up, with even the likes of Rupert Murdoch heaping praise on him, it was time for Sugar to reach for the Sky.

CHAPTER FIVE
SKY HIGH

The cultural significance and impact of the launch of Sky television can scarcely be overestimated. Quite simply, the experience of the television viewer would never be the same again. It was very much a launch that chimed with Sugar in both a business and leisure sense. He had long felt that British viewers were poorly served, particularly when compared with their American equivalent. There were just four channels for British viewers to choose from at this point, whereas in America there were more than 50 on offer. High on the list of Brits who would appreciate more television choice were what he saw as the classic Amstrad customer: the ordinary man and woman. 'Satellite broadcasting is good for our type of British consumer,' he said. 'It may not appeal to you lot [City analysts], but the *Sun* readership and the *News of the World* readership are going to buy that stuff.'

There was clearly serious money to be made here and the Amstrad customer was going to hand over a lot of it. 'US-Style TV Turns On Europe' ran the headline in *Fortune* magazine. So, when Rupert Murdoch knocked on Amstrad's door to see if they were interested in making the satellite dishes that would receive all these new channels, Sugar jumped into action. He gave Bob Watkins three days to find out if they could profitably make such dishes at the sale price Murdoch wanted: £199. Watkins reported back that, yes, this was a 'goer'. However, Sugar needed further reassurance from Murdoch before doing the deal. 'I put my humble hat on and said, "Look, I'm only a little humble lad from Brentwood. I haven't got the multi-mega-millions of your organisation. You're not asking me to ponce around making 5,000 pieces; you want me to put hundreds of thousands of receivers out there. So what happens if the bleeding rocket doesn't go up?"' Sugar also stressed that he wanted to get involved only if Sky could promise to launch at least four channels, including a movie channel. Sugar knew his television: he was an open fan of 'American garbage'.

With basic terms agreed within 21 days of Murdoch's first phone call to Sugar, the Amstrad boss set out to make a million satellite dishes in one year. The deal was announced at a press conference on 8 June 1988. Just two years previously, Sugar had stood alongside Sir Clive Sinclair in front of the press. Here, he stood alongside the mighty Rupert Murdoch. Without a word being spoken, here alone was evidence of how much Sugar was on the up. Murdoch boasted, 'We will be bringing for the first time real choice of viewing to the British and European public, particularly the British public. We are seeing the dawn of an age of freedom for viewing and freedom for advertising.'

Turning to the dishes manufacturing for which he had teamed up with Sugar, Murdoch said the venture would prove to be 'a major job-creation exercise'. Sugar agreed: 'It is our intention to manufacture these dishes and assemble the units in the UK. It would be very nice if we could manufacture them in an area of high unemployment. It is our intention to put our manufacturing process in that direction. At the moment, satellite television dishes on the UK market are selling for more than £1,000 and consumers are being asked to pay up to £200 for aerial erection. Those days are fast coming to an end. Our 60-centimetre dish, no bigger than an opened umbrella, does not need planning consent and will be erected by television aerial contractors for £40 or so.'

Turning to the man alongside him, Sugar said how pleased he and Amstrad were to be working with him of all people on this project. 'We are pleased that Rupert Murdoch has taken the initiative on this front. He has a reputation of getting things done and his proposal . . . is very exciting.'

He was asked how their project for dishes was progressing.

'We are starting to tool up for dishes and receivers,' he replied. 'Deliveries will start in the first quarter of 1989 at the rate of about 100,000 per month. We hope to set up a subcontractor in a high-unemployment area for UK assembly.' It was when he turned to the retail price for the dishes that Sugar drew gasps of admiration. For the Amstrad price was several times smaller than many would have expected.

'The Amstrad Fidelity 8RX 100 lead-in model will retail at £199 including VAT,' he revealed. 'Also there will be a series of enhanced models including a £259 unit with infrared remote control and a number of other features.' In distributing and selling the goods, Sugar would be drawing on Amstrad's extensive and impressive contacts book, he explained to the media throng. 'Distribution of the Amstrad Fidelity equipment will be made through the company's traditional high-street and independent stores and initial indications from some of our leading customers suggest that they are as excited about the opportunities as we are.' This much, then, was familiar territory.

However, this was the first time Amstrad had been properly involved in satellite television. Not that this would be its last involvement, predicted the boss. 'Although our first entry into satellite television will be through the dish and receiver sector, it should be noted that our Amstrad Fidelity brand is well placed to manufacture television sets and combined television/video units with built-in receivers. This is an area of the market we are studying now.'

Murdoch outlined just how significant he felt the launch of Sky was. 'This expansion of television presents great opportunities for a lot of people and organisations: viewers, advertisers, programme makers, electronics retailers and manufacturers,' he said. 'It also means new jobs across a range of industries.'

Turning to what Sky would actually offer the viewing public, he sold the service very well. 'The variety of quality programmes available will range from a wide choice of arts programmes to sporting events from around the world, to instant news coverage and to a wider selection of general entertainment. The film channel, which will be available in the UK only, will offer an extensive range of top movies from major distributors and they will be free of cost to the viewer.'

Many were excited by the prospect of Sky television, and the media were awash with stories about satellite television and how it would change all of our lives. 'Beaming Murdoch launches a battle for the skies' ran the headline in the following day's *Guardian*. True, in time, some of the non-Murdoch press would take great delight in poking fun at the Sky service, but at this point in the story it seemed that everyone was excited by this broadcasting revolution. And there was Sugar, the boy from Hackney, right in the middle of the action. Sugar's part in the revolution was to get those receiver dishes made – and fast. For this, he turned to the General Electric Company (GEC), whose managing director Lord Weinstock was no stranger to Sugar. The talks between Amstrad and GEC actually hit a rock at one point, and there were fears that the deal would not be done. Sugar decided to go straight to Lord Weinstock and warn him that the deal was on the rocks. 'I told him what was going on and that GEC was about to lose the order,' he explains. They tied up the details and the deal was struck. It reminded them of their dealings in the past. 'He liked doing the deal,' said Sugar. 'It reminded him of his early days, because him and me were haggling on the phone over 50 pence, which is probably something he hasn't done for 30 years.'

Of course, Sugar had been no fan of British electronics manufacturers in general prior to this. So he may have felt a little nervous about giving the dishes contract to a domestic firm. However, he was impressed with the outcome. 'I must give them credit where credit's due,' he said of the speed at which the GEC team worked. 'It brought back a lot of my confidence in British electronics when I saw them do that.' Once more, he was showing an openness to new ideas, to change. The man who once said that he wouldn't manufacture at home because he was running a business, not a benevolent society, was now not only using but praising British manufacturers.

Later, even more of Amstrad's manufacturing would 'come home'. In early 1999, Amstrad moved production of nearly a fifth of its PC2000 computer to a plant in Fife, Scotland. This plant was owned by GEC, and, by moving production there, Sugar saved 700 workers from losing their jobs. Sugar had worked out that, although it cost around £10 extra to make these products in the UK, the flexibility it allowed him in terms of reacting quickly to market trends more than made up for that. Accordingly, later that year he awarded the contract to produce Amstrad fax machines to a factory in Northern Ireland. This meant that around a quarter of Amstrad products were now made in Europe, rather than the Far East. He said this proportion of domestic production would increase in time. 'The Far East has no advantage any more in computers, because in the past the most labour-intensive part was the building and testing of the main printed-circuit board. Now, with automation and modern surface mount technology, that does not require so much labour.'

Returning to the Sky issue, Sugar was concerned that Murdoch may have viewed him as a 'geezer with a bloody great big head'. He was concerned that his knowledge, confidence and impulsive responses may paint him as a bighead. However, Sugar had simply felt that the News International people were entering a territory – electronics – where he knew far more than they did. Therefore, when Murdoch expressed his concern to Sugar that their rivals BSB might launch first, Sugar told him flat that they wouldn't. (He was right.) He also told Murdoch that the other electronics firms who were offering to make dishes wouldn't deliver on time. When the pair discussed how to best scramble the movie channel so only those paying for it would receive it, Sugar suggested using a smart card. Murdoch believed this would be too expensive, but ultimately backed down when his own technical experts backed up Sugar's view. 'Don't start barking like an old crow and shouting your head off, but basically you were right,' he told Sugar. 'We're going with the smart card.' However, he didn't hire Amstrad to make the smart cards, choosing to go with a rival firm instead. They'll deliver late, Sugar told Murdoch – and again he was right.

However, ultimately the various parts all came together and Sky was ready for launch. With Murdoch's newspapers regularly promoting the new service, demand began to pick up. 'People are driving us barmy wanting the dishes,' said Sugar. Here, his son Daniel gave an early indication that he had inherited his father's eye for a deal when he booked a hall in Essex on the night that Sky televised the Mike Tyson versus Frank Bruno fight and charged people £30 apiece to watch the fight and eat a meal. It turned out to be a nice little earner for Daniel, who was then just 18.

Meanwhile, Sky's rivals BSB struggled from embarrassment to disaster and back again. Sugar watched this as a particularly interested party because he had nearly got involved with them a few years previously. He could afford a smile when he realised that he had once again been proved right. He noted, though, with disdain that, despite BSB's woes, the City did not treat them with the same paranoia they had sometimes exhibited towards Amstrad. He joked that he was going to commission a sculptor to build a huge cement hand giving the famous two-finger salute. He would then, he quipped, get it placed right in the middle of the City. No Christmas card for the City analysts that year, then.

But what was the legacy of his involvement with Murdoch for Sugar himself? He said he suspected that, within two years of Sky's launch, Murdoch would have forgotten all about him. But Murdoch was more impressed with Sugar than that. 'I call him once or twice a month to see how things are going – to keep in touch and get his opinion on the marketplace,' he said after the launch of Sky had been and gone. Murdoch was very impressed with Sugar, and there was no evidence he considered him a bighead. Instead, he was gushing with praise. 'He's very entrepreneurial, a tremendous worker. In negotiations, he's a master of detail. I found he came to the point, to the bottom line very quickly. He's been very straight with me – totally. He's kept his word on everything.'

Might they work together again? 'I'd be surprised if there aren't other things we do with him,' Murdoch said with a smile. It would prove to be a very big deal when Murdoch's words eventually came true. Before then, there was much water to pass under the bridge – and not all of it was to be happy.

Every business and every businessperson goes through a rough patch. From the world's richest men to the modest small-business owner, everybody has ups and downs. However, it is at times such as these that the men get separated from the boys. There are those who respond defensively and there are those who react well, and Sugar belongs firmly in the second camp. The late 1980s became, in many ways, a bad time indeed for Amstrad, which lost £114 million in sales because it did not have the products to meet the demand. Its foreign subsidiaries began to perform less than ideally, and its share value collapsed. Dark times for his company, but Sugar did what every successful person does at such times: he analysed what had gone wrong and worked out what could be done about it. This may sound an obvious response to make, but the business world is full of people who were too busy stroking their own egos to have found their way out of trouble.

So you can imagine the surprise of the City analysts when they turned up at Amstrad's headquarters in Brentwood in February 1999 to find Sugar neither defensive nor in denial about his company's plight. Amstrad and the City had never enjoyed a close relationship, so, when the chips were down for the former, many of the latter would have been overjoyed at the chance to rub it in. Their defiance will not have been dampened by the fact that rail delays meant their journey out to Essex had been less than straightforward.

Sugar showed them in and went about explaining why pretax profits for the six months to the end of 1988 were down 16 per cent to £75.3 million. He was not about to attempt to put any glossy spins on this. Quite simply, he said, he wanted to call the financial year 'the year of disaster'. True, his advisers had suggested that this was not a sensible term to employ, but that did not stop Sugar from using it in front of the assembled City throng. His honest, open style was matched by Amstrad's marketing director Malcolm Miller, who sat next to Sugar at the gathering. 'We've been critical of ourselves,' said Miller. 'We've tried to understand what went wrong, so we can decide what to do.'

As mentioned, one of the major factors behind this dramatic drop in profits was that Amstrad was unable to supply the demand for its goods, which was largely due to a hike in the price of microchips. Amstrad tried to keep a flow of the microchips necessary to build its computers, printers and so on. However, at times during this dark period it was being forced to pay what Sugar called 'blackmail prices'. Eventually, Sugar paid for a stake in a company that produced microchips in the hope of securing a regular flow of them. This decision was lauded by the *Wall Street Journal*, who called it a 'wise investment'. However, even here things were to turn sour for Sugar. Soon after his investment, the problems that were forcing up the prices of microchips began to evaporate, wiping much of the value off the investment, which Sugar later acknowledged 'was not the greatest deal I've done'.

Meanwhile, over in Taiwan, labour shortages were slowing down the production of audio goods, and the production of video recorders was also failing to move quickly enough. Problems with the West German distribution of computers did little to help make the picture any brighter. 'Nineteen eighty-eight was planned to be the first year that Amstrad Germany was to show a major contribution to the group result,' said Sugar. 'I am sorry to say that in the first half this did not go according to plan . . . we accept in hindsight that this situation was self-inflicted.' Drawing to a conclusion, Sugar was honest yet upbeat. 'We made some bad mistakes. I don't really know why so many things went wrong at the one time. But, come the new financial year, we will be firing on all cylinders again.' Sugar had performed brilliantly at the meeting, but even his greatest performance could not stop Amstrad from taking a kicking at the City. That day the share price fell 12 per cent, knocking £57 million off the value of his personal stake in the company.

This time, the *Wall Street Journal* was less positive, running a story headed: 'Amstrad takes humbling turn for Alan Sugar'. *The Times* echoed this, reporting that:

'Profits tumble to £75 million after Amstrad "mistakes"'. Martin Waller's story read, 'Amstrad, the consumer electronics group, saw £125 million wiped off its market capitalisation yesterday after reporting a year-on-year pre-tax profits drop for the first time in its history.' Meanwhile, the *Independent* sneered, 'Things turn sour for Sugar'.

At least the *Guardian* noted that Sugar was responding to these sour times with a sensible head: 'Sugar owns up, and doesn't try to sweeten the pill,' wrote Roger Cowe. His fair report went on, 'Seldom are chairmen's statements of interest except to students of public relations. It is always interesting to see what depths can be represented as "a firm foundation for future growth" and what windfalls are credited to clear strategy and professional management. But company chairmen are not supposed to tell the truth – or certainly not the whole truth.

'All credit, then, to Amstrad founder and chairman Alan Sugar for owning up to a series of mistakes which have led to his company making the worst kind of history by reporting a drop in profits for the first time. Of course Mr Sugar is in a slightly more comfortable position than most company chairmen, since he still owns nearly half the company. And he has always been one to speak his mind, usually at the expense of his City critics. But even so, his frankness is surprising as well as more than welcome, and worthy of extensive quotation: "The result is below our expectations and our true potential due to a chain of events, some outside our control and others the results of our own mistakes."'

However, none of this could hide the fact that Amstrad had gone through a bad period, and had done so in front of the eyes of the world. As the *Economist* magazine concluded, 'Amstrad's Alan Sugar has not exactly tripped, but he is limping.' He would soon be back in his normal confident stride, but not before a major legal battle.

Amstrad had launched itself selling audio equipment, but, by the end of the 1980s, such goods had become a minority concern. Indeed, in 1989, audio sales contributed to less than 4 per cent of the company's turnover. 'There's no margin left in the product and we're just wasting our time chasing it,' he commented. Taking a long, hard look at the structure of his company, he added, 'We have had such phenomenal growth over the past few years that we are still operating with a management team you would expect to be running a company a fraction of our size,' he admitted to the *Sunday Times*. He also said that there was 'no financial policing within the organisation'. All of this was to change, not least because he appointed new directors to the board to address these and other matters. He also appointed a group inventory controller to keep a tighter rein on stock. As Sugar said, Amstrad was not carrying out 'mundane and boring tasks' that were required from a company such as his. Another change he ushered in during this testing era was a new dawn in customer service. To this end, 111,000-square-foot premises in Harlow, Essex, were purchased and crammed full of customer-service operatives who sat at their phones, answering questions from customers and computer dealers. Director Jim Rice said he saw this development as 'a very important aspect of our future strategy, and it's going to be developed much more than it currently is'.

Another part of their strategy was taken up by a lengthy legal battle with a US company. On 16 September 1991, Amstrad announced that it was suing electronics firm Seagate, seeking 'in excess of $150m compensation for financial loss caused to Amstrad and loss caused to Amstrad's reputation as a result of delivery of ST277R Hard Disc Drives' (for Amstrad's PC2386 personal computers), which, Amstrad alleged, 'were initially defective and had to be reworked by Seagate'. Seagate said it would vigorously defend the action, which it said was 'without merit'. The resulting poor quality of the PC2386 and its sister computer, the PC2286, damaged Amstrad's reputation in the early 1990s. It was a costly and lengthy battle, but, eventually, in May 1997, Amstrad won £57 million in damages. Judge Humphrey Lloyd, QC, the official referee for the case, ruled that the disk drives made by Seagate had been faulty and awarded damages to Amstrad under the Sale of Goods Act.

A relieved Sugar said, 'Nobody will ever know where Amstrad would be today if this had not happened. The great efforts of myself and my small team were demolished. The financial award we have received today only goes some way to compensate us.'

Seagate said they were stunned. 'I was shocked and appalled,' said their coincidentally named chief executive Alan Shugart. 'I think we got home-courted.'

The media were quick to pick up on the significance of all this. 'Amstrad hits the legal jackpot', cheered the *Guardian*. The accompanying story on the City page outlined that this victory had far-reaching consequences for Amstrad. 'The fortunes of Amstrad, Alan Sugar's struggling electronics company, were transformed yesterday by a surprise court victory which will boost the company's value by nearly half. Amstrad won a decision in a case dating back to the late 1980s which will bring the once high-flying computer company a windfall of more than £100 million in damages and interest.'

It had been a bitter battle for the man with a sweet surname. However, his involvement in the beautiful game was to lead to more than a few ugly moments, too.

CHAPTER SIX

COME ON, YOU SPURS!

Tottenham Hotspur has always been a football club that considers itself to be a bit different, a bit special. Founded in 1882 as Hotspur FC, with the motto *Audere est Facere* ('To dare is to do'), it has an illustrious history, and a reputation that actually exceeds its achievements. Not that it is entirely short of achievements. It became the first British club to win the domestic double in the 20th century. This came in the 1960/61 season, when Bill Nicholson guided the team to the League title and FA Cup. Then, in 1963, Tottenham became the first British club to win a major European trophy, the European Cup Winners Cup.

The 1980s was also a good decade for the side, who won the FA Cup twice, the FA Charity Shield and the UEFA Cup. However, even when Tottenham have not been winning trophies – and recent times have been mostly lean in that regard – they have managed to maintain a reputation as a stylish club, with a team who play stylish football. Such football royalty as Danny Blanchflower, Jimmy Greaves, Glenn Hoddle, Chris Waddle, Gary Lineker and Ossie Ardiles have turned out in their colours. So too have Pat Jennings, Jürgen Klinsmann and Teddy Sheringham.

In the early 1990s, a slump in the property market had left the then owner Irving Scholar – and therefore the club – in financial turmoil. Scholar was a lifelong Tottenham fan. As a boy he had dreamed of playing for Spurs, and he went as close as he could to fulfilling that dream by buying the club in 1982. The club was £4 million in debt, and Scholar appointed Douglas Alexiou as chairman. However, his ambitions for the club to become a global power were not realised, and instead Tottenham was heading towards financial disaster.

Before long, Scholar began to try to raise funds to bail out the club. In July 1989, he approached newspaper publisher and Derby County chairman Robert Maxwell in a bid for financial backing. However, in due course Maxwell would attempt to go even further than this. This attempt would put him on a head-to-head course with Sugar, who, though not a football fanatic like Scholar, had had connections with the north London giants on more than one occasion in the past. As a youngster, he had been taken to watch Spurs play at White Hart Lane by his father. Later, in the 1980s, the Amstrad office was in Garman Road, a mere goal kick away from Tottenham Hotspur's stadium. Furthermore, he had once used the Tottenham team in an advertising campaign for Amstrad. So he was no stranger to the team.

However, in the 1990s these connections would be mere trailers to the main feature: Alan Sugar would buy Tottenham Hotspur Football Club. In June 1991, Sugar teamed up with Spurs legend Terry Venables to bid to buy the club from the departing Scholar.

As a player, Venables had enjoyed a successful career. He left school in 1957 and joined Chelsea FC as an apprentice. Three years later, he became a first-team regular and ultimately club captain. With him wearing the armband, Chelsea came agonisingly close to winning silverware a few times before they did finally hit the jackpot, winning the League Cup in 1965. Within a year, he had fallen out with manager Tommy Docherty and he was sold to Tottenham Hotspur, where he again tasted success, in the shape of an FA Cup final defeat of his old club Chelsea.

After retiring as a player, Venables turned to management, and he guided Crystal Palace to two successive promotions; he then moved across town to Queens Park Rangers whom he led to the Division Two title. By now, this hot young managerial ace was attracting widespread global attention in the game. Indeed, so high was his stock that he was approached by one of the game's most prestigious clubs: FC Barcelona.

He quickly accepted their offer and found himself swapping the small, tight surroundings of Queens Park Rangers' Loftus Road stadium for the sprawling majestic splendour of the Camp Nou, where he earned the nickname 'El Tel'. The charismatic Venables would not disappoint. He steered the club to their first League title in 11 years, a League Cup win and a European Cup Final, which they lost on penalties to Steaua Bucharest.

However, such was his reputation and success that El Tel found it hard to live up to his early glories at the club, and, in fact, he became a victim of his own success. By the time his side lost to Dundee United in the UEFA Cup, his time was up and he was sacked.

Within eight weeks, he was back in work, this time at the helm of Tottenham Hotspur, the team of his playing days. It was here that he was destined to cross paths with Sugar. However, it is instructive to understand the full character of Venables in order to comprehend fully what subsequently unfolded.

A man who has had widespread business interests for many years, Venables has often been surrounded by controversy. He vigorously denies allegations of financial impropriety that have been made against him in the past. That said, he was banned from holding company directorships for seven years after choosing to not contest nineteen specific allegations made against him by the Department of Trade and Industry (DTI). The DTI case arose from alleged mismanagement of four companies –

the London drinking club Scribes West Ltd, Edenote plc, Tottenham Hotspur plc and Tottenham Hotspur Football and Athletic Company Ltd. Venables was not at the London courtroom where Elizabeth Gloster QC, for the DTI, told Mr Justice Evans-Lombe that his conduct in relation to the four companies 'has been such as to make him unfit to be concerned in any way with the management of a company'. The Competition and Consumer Affairs Minister Nigel Griffiths reacted to the verdict thus: 'Mr Venables has admitted the serious allegations made in the disqualification proceedings and recognises the serious nature of the allegations by consenting to a substantial seven-year period of disqualification. We recognise his great achievement in football coaching, but even our national heroes cannot be allowed to fall below accepted standards of probity when they enter the business world.'

Venables has also become famous away from the world of football, having co-authored four novels with author Gordon Williams and co-created a television series for ITV. He has also created a football board game and appeared on a pop song. All this, together with his perma-tanned appearance and hugely charismatic cockney persona, has long helped to cast Venables as one of the more colourful characters in the game. He was at the helm when England reached the semifinals of the 1996 European Championships, which remains to date the joint-second (with the 1990 World Cup run) most successful tournament performance the national side have managed since winning the World Cup in the glorious year of 1966.

However, much of that was yet to come when Venables and Sugar – who had for a while been associates but not what one would call friends – approached Spurs with their bid. After much speculation, Sugar revealed that there had indeed been a bid. 'I can't deny that Terry and I have made an approach to the board of Tottenham Hotspur and we are awaiting the outcome of that offer,' admitted Sugar. Referring to rumours that Robert Maxwell was also preparing a bid, Sugar made it clear how he saw proceedings panning out were there to be a bid to rival his and Venables's. 'If Mr Maxwell or any other party wish to come along for the benefit of the club and put forward proposals which are better than I am, I will gracefully step to one side, because one thing that is not going to happen is an auction,' he said.

Maxwell was indeed close to putting forward a proposal. Accordingly, his staff were alerted to the imminent sale of Derby County FC to Peter Gadsby, a property developer from the Peak District. Maxwell planned to take the £4 million he would earn from the sales of the recently relegated Midlands club, add to it the £40 million he had also garnered from the recent *Daily Mirror* flotation, and buy a significant shareholding in Spurs. As these rumours gathered pace, Sugar came out fighting again. Drawing on his expert salesman abilities, he made sure that the advantages of a Sugar–Venables bid were spelled out via the media. 'I've got a cheque in the fridge and Terry Venables and I are ready to go as soon as the board sorts itself out,' asserted salesman Sugar. 'We put serious proposals to the board on Monday and I believe that, with Terry's undisputed talent and history of success, when combined with my financial backing, the future prospects for Spurs are excellent.' It did indeed seem at the time an attractive prospect when compared with that of Robert Maxwell. A dream ticket, one could say.

Although the tale was going to end bitterly, with the benefit of hindsight it must still be a relief to Spurs fans that Maxwell did not win the day.

As time went on, Sugar upped the stakes and piled a bit more pressure on the club. He had clearly been swotting up on the laws and rules of the Football League. Once more presenting himself to the media, Sugar gave chapter and verse on what he saw as the flaws in Maxwell's north London ambitions. 'We have heard a lot of noise about another possible bid for Spurs,' said Sugar. 'Our reading of the concisely written League rules means that, even if Derby are sold, Robert Maxwell still cannot bid for Spurs. His family holding in Oxford and Reading would have to be disposed of first, unless the League gives written dispensation.'

But would the League be of a mind to give such dispensation? Sugar's answer was unequivocal. 'I cannot believe that the League could find sufficient reason to do so in the light of our solid bid and the known feelings of the fans, players and many small shareholders, all of whom desperately want Terry Venables to stay on.' Once more, the salesman was showing his skills. Here he had charmingly but pointedly pressurised the League to come round to his way of thinking. This was as good a combination of soft and hard sell as one could imagine in the circumstances, and it was soon backed up by the very people Sugar had alluded to in his statement.

The Tottenham Independent Supporters' Club told the media that a bid from Robert Maxwell would be 'unacceptable' to them, and they backed up Sugar's belief that such a bid would breach Football League rules because of his interests in Oxford, Reading and Manchester United. Coordinator Bernie Kingsley said, 'We would be prepared to take legal advice to seek an injunction if it seemed the League was going to break its own rules.'

Sugar must have smiled broadly when he read these quotes. With so much united pressure, things could only tip his way. The media seemed to favour the Sugar–Venables camp too. The headline in the *Guardian* newspaper was typical: 'Alan Sugar's bid may save Spurs'. In the accompanying story, it became clear that Sugar's claim that he and El Tel had the support of shareholders was spot on. Frank Sinclair, one of Tottenham's executive directors, told the newspaper, 'We are pleased about any bid that's likely to be successful.

The club has received numerous approaches over the last nine months, but the important thing is to have one that is likely to have a successful outcome. Mr Sugar has considerable financial muscle.' He did indeed. Sugar was at this point worth £157 million, and had recently been placed at 46th in the *Sunday Times Rich List*.

An unnamed boardroom source was equally positive about Sugar, telling the *Independent*'s veteran football reporter Joe Lovejoy, 'For the first time in many months of negotiation, Venables has finally come up with someone who has got the money involved. Alan Sugar is a very bright fellow. We can do business with him.'

Back then, football was not considered the valuable financial cash cow that it is now. So, although there was backing for Sugar, there was some uncertainty as to what was attracting him to make such a bid. 'Who knows?' the same source said, shrugging, when asked. 'Maybe he's got tired of computer games and wants a new toy. He can afford it.'

As for Sugar, he was clear about the attraction of the deal. 'Look, this is the fourth time I've told you,' he told one persistent inquisitor. 'It's a business proposition, and a very good business proposition.'

Sugar carried on heaping on the pressure via the media. 'We have made a proposal and obviously on the basis of that proposal we hope that the club will be back on a reasonable financial ground in the future,' Sugar told a journalist. Once more, he played his trump card:

the involvement of the popular Terry Venables. 'I think the supporters will really be very, very pleased that Terry Venables is still involved with the club. I think that is the key issue.'

The pressure eventually told, and the deal was finally done. On Saturday, 22 June, Sugar and Venables called a triumphant press conference to announce that they had reached agreement with the board of Tottenham Hotspur and the Stock Exchange to purchase the shares of Irving Scholar and Paul Bobroff, and were assuming control of the north London giants. Under the new regime, Sugar would become nonexecutive chairman of the plc with the task of 'getting the balance sheet into shape', while Venables would take over the role of managing director. The first thing that Sugar and Venables did was pay off the club's £20 million debt. It seemed a match made in heaven, but – to borrow a football parlance – it would well and truly kick off.

Perhaps it was clear all along that Sugar and Venables would struggle to work together. They certainly made for a high-charisma pairing. 'Terry is all charm, he could persuade you that black is white,' said a business source who has dealt with both. 'Alan is gruff and aggressive. But both have monster egos and their self-belief is rarely shaken.'

A journalist in the *Daily Mail* pointed out one major difference between the two men. True, Venables had a greater football pedigree than Sugar. But this deal was as much to do with business as the beautiful game and, wrote the journalist, 'In this world, Alan Michael Sugar is AC Milan. And Terry Venables is Halifax Town.' The 'Halifax Town' of the deal would later look back and conclude that, while he had made 'plenty of mistakes' in his career, this one was the worst.

On taking the reins at White Hart Lane, Sugar made clear how his and Venables's duties were divided. 'Terry will look after the 11 players on the field, I'll take care of the £11 million at the bank,' he said. The figure was not just to make a convenient soundbite, as Sugar explained, 'This club was heading for the receivers when I came along. It owed the Midland Bank £11 million.'

Accordingly, soon after the two took control, Sugar underwrote a fresh injection of money, making him the dominant investor. Soon, however, the partnership went sour. In 1993, Sugar sacked Venables. In business, tough decisions have to be taken and this was a tough decision indeed, for the charismatic Venables was widely adored by the Tottenham faithful and the football community in general. Looking back at how and why he summoned the courage to part company with Venables, Sugar was as concise and direct as ever: 'Terry: clever man, wise man, smart fellow, written books, loved by the fans. Some people would have said, "No, I'm, not gonna take on God's gift." But I made a statement: I was in, up to here. Terry Venables was out. I made that statement to the world at large, to my family, to me.'

The decision had been taken at a two-hour board meeting. The conclusion of the board meeting was that Sugar pointed his finger at Venables and said, 'You're fired.'

Venables emerged shaken, saying simply, 'The board has voted to dismiss me, and I have been and am talking to solicitors. I am advised that's all I can say at the moment.'

So what had prompted Sugar's brave decision? He was clear that it was not connected to football matters. After all, Venables had guided the club to the FA Cup semifinal that season, where only a late header from Tony Adams of Arsenal had prevented the club from reaching their second FA Cup final in two years. Instead, he said, it was due to associates of Venables. 'Nobody is questioning his ability as a football coach. And it was a very sad day on Friday, and everybody involved regrets deeply that it has come to this.' He added that, although many of the fans would be upset to see Venables go, it was the correct thing to do and that they would soon agree. 'Obviously fans want the team to be strong; they want good management of the football side. We have got good management there at the moment, which worked under Terry Venables – Doug Livermore and Ray Clemence.

'We will apply the funds in an appropriate manner that one should apply cash in a football club. And the playing will tell the story. Fans are very fickle. There is a distinct possibility that three or four games into the season, if we win and the manager becomes a hero, the cruel harsh reality is that maybe, maybe Terry is forgotten.' He later added, 'I'd like to say to the fans that I and the board have the best interests of the club at heart. This is not an ego trip – I'm not an egotistical loony. If I was I'd have been reported many times before for interfering in football. This club has been established since 1882. It's bigger than me, it's bigger than Robert Maxwell and it's bigger than Terry Venables.'

All the same, he had not heard the last of the matter. Venables took the case to the High Court, applying for an injunction against his dismissal. The judge ruled that reinstating Venables would 'merely postpone the date at which all concerned must face up to the fact that his appointment, for better or worse, has been terminated'.

Spurs fans were furious, and chanted, 'We want Sugar out' outside the court. Sugar was escorted out of a back door, and has since said that, in firing Venables, he felt as if he had murdered Bambi.

As for Venables, he has been surprisingly conciliatory since. 'I don't know what would have happened to the club without him,' he has acknowledged. 'He was the only one prepared to go through with it.'

Nonetheless, the whole battle had been a bitter one for everyone who loved Tottenham Hotspur. An even more terrifying challenge was soon to land on the club's doorstep. The FA had for some time been holding an investigation into alleged illegal payments that the club had made to players during the 1980s, long before the involvement of either Sugar or Venables. With that investigation completed in the summer of 1994, the club were found guilty and given an extraordinary punishment: 12 League points deducted for the 1994/95 Premier League season, a one-year ban from FA Cup competition, and a £600,000 fine. Many saw this punishment as essentially guaranteeing the club not just a trophyless season for 1994/95, but also a relegation season. This was a disaster. The club statement hardly began to hint at the distress in the air in the white and blue sector of north London: 'The board of Tottenham Hotspur is extremely disappointed and unhappy at yesterday's decision by the Football Association, and is considering options available to it, and will make a decision by the end of next week as to what action, if any, to take.'

The decision was naturally taken to appeal to an arbitration panel. The response of the appeal was a mixed blessing. The fine was increased to a record £1.5 million, the FA Cup ban was upheld but the points deduction was reduced from twelve to six.

Sugar's mood at this time was not helped by the fact that he had just gone into hospital for an operation on both shoulders. All the same, he came out fighting and upbeat. 'We're not going down now,' he told reporters referring to the moderation of the points deduction. 'We have just lost two games, that's all. Looking on the positive side, when Arsenal had points deducted in 1991, they went on to win the Championship. The players we are considering buying should not see this as too much of an obstacle.'

However, this look-on-the-bright-side talk should not be mistaken for any approval on Sugar's part of the fact that the financial penalty had been made tougher after the appeal. 'I find that laughable,' he said. 'I am shell-shocked. The money is a joke.' He was also quite naturally upset that the Cup ban had been upheld, not least given Tottenham's fine record in knockout competitions. 'I was hoping we would be allowed back into the FA Cup. We've always been known as a Cup team. I was also hoping they might have suspended the points sentence, like they did the penalties they imposed on Millwall for crowd trouble.'

FA spokesman Glen Kirton said he understood that Tottenham would be unhappy with the situation. 'However, the board considered the charges which were admitted to be very serious matters,' he added. 'These breaches of rules were evidence of a practice adopted at the club for many years, which resulted in an advantage over others who had complied with the rules. Mr Sugar gave us a personal assurance, that we are happy to accept, that there will be no repetition of this type of conduct at the club.'

Sugar did not only have to offer an assurance to the FA: he also had to try to reassure staff and supporters. Then manager Argentinian Ossie Ardiles was said to be taking it on the chin. 'Ossie's getting up off the floor now,' said Sugar after the appeal. 'He's disappointed about the FA Cup but he now knows he hasn't got a problem as far as relegation is concerned.'

The manager himself backed up this upbeat message. 'Look, let me make one thing clear in all this,' said Ardiles. 'I have no time for self-pity. We have a lot of talented players here and some potentially very good players. Sometimes people think it is all gloom and doom around here and that just isn't the case. I have been very impressed with the attitude of the boys. They have been positive and that is what I wanted.'

A second appeal was filed and in November 1994 the appeal tribunal issued the following statement: 'The arbitration tribunal convened to hear the challenge by Tottenham Hotspur FC to the Football Association's punishment has decided to remit the matter to a new FA Commission. Spurs' punishment, and in particular, its participation in this season's FA Cup, is dependent on the decision of the new commission. Reasons for the tribunal's findings will be given to the parties shortly.'

Could it be that the club could possibly go one better, with a second appeal to the FA? They could if Sugar had his way, and he piled the pressure on the authorities by reminding them that Tottenham were not the only club with skeletons in their closet. 'I don't want to be dragged down to the levels of depravity which may exist in the football industry in hiding or covering up things. So I hope the private arbitration in this case will find for honesty, because that's always the best policy,' he said.

Turning the screw on the football authorities, he added, 'But, I'm sorry, if the tribunal holds up what the Football Association has done, I will use my best endeavours on behalf of the shareholders of my club to disclose the same irregularities by other clubs, it doesn't matter who they are. I make that quite clear because, if we are treated that way, and I find it has happened at other clubs, they should be treated the same.'

This was a quite justifiable public stance to take. Football was beset by corruption at the time, and Tottenham could quite justifiably feel they were being made a scapegoat. Furthermore, Sugar was not at the club when the offences took place, so he could feel very aggrieved at being punished.

Around this time, he was asked what would constitute a successful season for the club. It is a mark of the horrendous situation the club were in at the time that his reply was not focused on on-field matters. 'Success for Spurs at the moment is to have no one suing us and no regulatory authority on our backs,' he said bluntly. 'That would do for starters.' Indeed, this was a candid interview by the Amstrad chief. 'I'm still learning,' he said of his part in the football world. 'This is my fourth season, the first two were with [Venables] and it's only the last two that I've been involved in every detail.' As he returned to the punishment issue, his anger quickly rose.

'To me, when you see the ratbags in football, it's commendable that there's a regulatory body like the Football Association which still holds it all together. But common sense tells you whatever Tottenham are supposed to be guilty of, if the same misdemeanour was perpetrated by Brighton and Hove Albion, there's no way they would have been fined £1.5 million.' He felt that the club were being punished especially heavily because of their wealth. 'I'm rich, OK, but, if I park my Rolls-Royce in Kensington, the fine is thirty quid, the same as it would be for someone with a bubble car. The FA have stuck a finger in the air and said, "Right, it's Tottenham, they've got plenty of money." Wallop!'

The second appeal was more successful: the points deduction and FA Cup ban were both withdrawn.

Sugar took this opportunity to outline once more how he saw the balance of power in the football club. Even for football purists, who feel uncomfortable at the role of 'money men' in the game – although how do they imagine the game would survive without money? – Sugar's case was impressive. 'My view is that the manager should identify the players he requires, then discuss them in confidence with the chairman, who does all the commercial negotiations. How can you expect a manager who has spent all his life learning how to kick a ball into a net to have any idea of finance and delicate negotiations?

'The only way you judge a manager is on results and the choice of players he asks the chairman to purchase for him. I wouldn't dream of telling Ossie which players to buy, but, if the man wasn't skilled or capable of doing the job, he'd be out.' Sugar also turned to his own image, which had taken something of a kicking during the Venables saga. Although the perception of Sugar is often unfair, he is aware of how many see him and is willing to articulately challenge his image. 'The rumours are that I'm so arrogant, so set in my ways, that I'm not prepared to admit I'm wrong,' he said. 'That's a load of balderdash. I'm known in the business world as a cut-and-run man. I'm not proud to admit to mistakes, but I've made them and I'm out before you know it.'

Looking back over the entire saga, he added, 'I've got faith in the truth, honesty and that straight dealing will out in the end. Believe me when I tell you that, if I hadn't volunteered the information about what happened here in the past, none of this would be happening to Spurs. I don't regret doing what I've done because that would be going against my nature. And if I was like the way I'm portrayed in the press – as this nasty villainous ogre, which has really upset me and my family – don't you think I would have been exposed by now?'

It's a very pertinent conclusion. In an era when the media are hugely probing and persistent, they have been unable to find any dirt against Sugar. Plenty of other successful businesspeople have been turned over in the media but not Sugar. Even though you can sense that some journalists would love nothing more than to spoil his party, they have been unable to. So they are forced to accept that his titanic business empire has been built with honest sweat and sharp thinking, rather than anything at all corrupt.

So too did Tottenham supporters come round to Sugar's way of thinking. Doubts about his commitment to the club were beginning to evaporate. As *Independent* journalist Norman Fox put it, 'Watch Sugar at a match now and you see a fan. Most chairmen wince a little when the opposition score and smile reservedly when their own team do so; Sugar grimaces and roars.'

Fox was far from alone in noticing this. The *Evening Standard*'s influential Michael Herd also picked up on it. 'What has happened to Alan Sugar? Has he picked up the Jack Walker virus and given himself up to football, body and soul?' asked Herd. 'Has Mr Grumpy got the bug despite everything he's seen and heard in the past three years? After all, it wasn't so long ago he was telling us his association with Tottenham was his single biggest mistake. He'd gone to White Hart Lane as a boy but since then he hadn't shown any interest in football.'

Herd's article was written after Sugar had just pulled off a deal that was to shock the football world, and would have the Tottenham faithful jumping for joy. Born in Göppingen in 1964, Jürgen Klinsmann is renowned as one of the best strikers of the modern era. His first major club was VfB Stuttgart, and it was there that Klinsmann became a prolific goal scorer, scoring an amazing 79 goals in 156 appearances. In 1988, he was top scorer of the Bundesliga and was voted 'German Player of the Year'. He hooked up with fellow German aces Lothar Matthäus and Andreas Brehme at Italian giants Inter Milan, who romped to the Serie A title. Klinsmann was ultimately to score 40 goals in 123 appearances in Italy. He then moved to France in 1992 to play for AS Monaco.

Meanwhile, he was becoming a major hit in the international scene, too. He was the first player ever to score at least three goals in each of three World Cups. Perhaps his best personal performance in this competition came in the 1994 World Cup, where he scored five goals. It was after this tournament finished that Sugar made his audacious move to bring this football sensation to White Hart Lane, in what was hailed by the *Daily Mail* as 'English football's transfer coup of the decade'.

It was indeed a shock for everyone to see Sugar shaking hands with Klinsmann on board his yacht in Monaco. Here was a man on top of his game, one of football's most talented and charismatic players, willing to join a mid-table English club that was at that stage staring down the barrel at a points deduction and Cup ban. Players like Klinsmann just didn't come to clubs like Tottenham, was the received wisdom. But since when has Sugar ever let received wisdom get between him and a good deal? And this was a good deal, indeed. A monumental one, in fact. Klinsmann promised to do for

Tottenham what Frenchman Eric Cantona had done for Manchester United. Such players were more than stars: they were talismans. Their presence, their charisma transformed teams. There was something little short of magical about them.

The effect of his signing was immediate. 'Klins-mania' broke out in north London. Tottenham fans were unable to believe their luck in acquiring his services, and Arsenal fans were soon looking nervously across the divide. Could it be that Sugar had pulled off a transfer that would ultimately see Tottenham emerge from the shadows of their illustrious neighbours and claim bragging rights for north London? Plenty thought so at the time! Michael Herd was quick to capture this mood, and to credit Sugar with a central role in the drama. 'Now, suddenly, we have a photograph of Sugar, looking rather self-satisfied, standing on his yacht with Klinsmann,' he wrote. 'The German has said "yes" and there is no doubt the Tottenham chairman and not the manager, Ossie Ardiles, has been the principal player. Sugar is happy to talk about the deal. A call had gone into his Brentwood office a few weeks earlier from Klinsmann's lawyer, a man named Andy Gross (a great name for a percentage man!) during which Sugar had learned the German was available.'

Herd paints a portrait of just how sharp and decisive a player Sugar was in this remarkable coup. '[Gross and Sugar] talk but decide to stay stumm until after the

World Cup, then Sugar does what would have been the unthinkable not long ago. He breaks into a sailing holiday to meet Klinsmann in Monte Carlo. The German visits the yacht on three consecutive days and the deal is done.'

Indeed, it was, and Sugar was quick to outline just how pleasurable it had been: 'Klinsmann and his lawyer were very straightforward. They liked everything clear on the table in front of them. You often don't get a chance to say to a player what a great club Tottenham are, their history and tradition. With Klinsmann we did. Jürgen was looking for a challenge and he decided that Tottenham was the one that interested him most. We've told him what we have got to do and we're delighted he has chosen our club to help us try to win something next year, and the year after.'

Although this story was like an earthquake across planet football, the actual ins and outs of the deal were fairly simple, as Sugar told reporters. 'We will be starting off with a two-year contract. We are going to London on Monday to have the usual fitness tests and on Monday we should be signed up.' What of the German? Klinsmann said it was the 'history and tradition' that Sugar had described to him that swung his affections towards north London. 'I had a couple of offers from Spain and Italy, but Tottenham is a very prestigious club with a lot of tradition and the Premier League is one of the best in Europe,' he said, grinning. 'I am very proud to play for the club and my immediate aim is to win something with Tottenham.'

Manager Ossie Ardiles felt like all his Christmases had come at once: 'This all proves the strength of Alan Sugar's commitment to the club. Our goal is to put Spurs on top, maybe not this season, but soon. Being in the middle is not good enough for us.' However, Ardiles drew the line at suggestions that this was the most important signing in the history of the club, claiming that particular honour for himself. Cheeky, but probably true.

But the Klinsmann capture would run a close second. Sugar's trusted adviser Nick Hewer expanded on how they got their man. 'Alan rang me from his yacht in Monaco at 7.30am and told me there was a good chance of signing Klinsmann,' said Hewer. 'He was very excited but the negotiations were at a delicate stage. It was touch and go for a time. The deal was concluded, after some particularly tough bargaining with Monaco, at around midday and Alan is obviously delighted about signing a player of such quality.

'Although he has been on holiday in the South of France, he has been on the telephone in his cabin for most of the time. He has masterminded the whole thing and kept in constant touch with Ossie the whole time.'

Confirming that there was plenty of opposition to their bid, Sugar said, 'We faced strong opposition from other clubs but were able to offer the right package to these players. Germany did not have a good World Cup but

Klinsmann himself had a very good tournament, scoring five goals. The signing . . . is something that we have been working on for a long, long time. Going forward, we are certainly going to be very, very strong.'

Strong indeed, for Klinsmann was not the only exciting capture of the summer. Ilie Dumitrescu had starred at the World Cup for Romania. Tricky and skilful, he had been one of the stars of the summer, a key spark in the team's march to the quarterfinals. He too signed on the dotted line. Reporters asked Ardiles how the club had managed to attract such stars at a time of uncertainty over the FA punishment, which was still active at this point. 'Of course, these players know about the FA Cup and the six points,' said Ardiles. 'They will help us make up the points. As Ilie said, it will mobilise us and it is only two wins.' Ardiles was clearly delighted at scooping everyone. He said, 'With Ilie we beat competition from other clubs including Bari, Padova and yesterday Atletico Madrid. Then we faced competition for Jürgen. He preferred to come to us because he likes English football and knows a surprising amount about it.'

English football knew plenty about Klinsmann, too. White Hart Lane legend Bill Nicholson, who was in charge when Spurs won the double in 1961, was enthralled at the capture of the German. He said, 'Klinsmann is 30 and at the peak of his career. He is a very experienced and consistent goal scorer who seems able to score against the best opposition and that is what we need.'

Nicholson's excitement was matched by the fans who worship him. As Tottenham Hotspur press officer Ashley Weller explained, 'Fans have been ringing up all afternoon asking whether it's really true. They can't believe it. It's going to make a big difference to season-ticket sales.'

It did indeed, as the ticket office staff were quick to confirm. 'The telephones have been red hot following the two signings,' said ticket office manager Chris Belt to waiting reporters. 'In a normal year we would hope to sell around 10,000 season tickets before the new season, but we will now expect to comfortably improve upon that.'

The club fully expected to bank more than £500,000 in season-ticket sales in three weeks and were confident that home games at White Hart Lane would be sell-outs throughout the campaign. The almost hysterical response to Klinsmann's signing also meant a flood of fans went through the doors of the club shops, to buy replica shirts with the striker's surname on them, and, suddenly, north London seemed to be full of Jürgen Klinsmanns.

Meanwhile, the bookmakers were taking note of the quality squad that Sugar had assembled, and reacting accordingly. 'Achtung! Bookies in Panic: Spurs odds are slashed after they sign £2m Klinsmann' yelped the headline in the *Daily Record*. 'Bookies have slashed Spurs title odds from 250–1 to 50–1 and expect to cut them further.'

Sugar's genius in the transfer market was once more laid bare: from relegation certainties to title contenders, all thanks to a couple of signings. True, some were getting a little carried away with the excitement of it all, but excitement was just what the club needed. Morale was rocketing, and Sugar was responsible.

The man himself was in buoyant and proud mood. 'No more Mr Nobodies will join this club,' he boasted at the press conference, where a relaxed and jovial Klinsmann was unveiled to the world's media. 'The FA have made it tough for us, and it is my kind of spirit to hit back and try to solve the problems. Rather than struggle, I prefer to try to throw money at the problems to try to solve them. It is in my character to fight fire with fire. These signings are my way of hitting back at our friends at Lancaster Gate.' Defiant and proud, this was Sugar at his best. After the tribulations of recent times, who would begrudge Sugar the chance to remind some of his critics of how he had proved them wrong? 'I came in for a lot of criticism last season, but I said I was not going to be panicked,' he explained. 'I said that when everyone was gunning for our manager Ossie Ardiles's head. You dig your heels in the ground and get on with it. If you do things in a professional and proper way, things will eventually come through. We have a plan and that plan is coming together.' But he was not about to get carried away by the hype. 'As for Spurs winning the Championship, I don't know so much about that. We are starting the season six points behind the others and we are not in the FA Cup. I thought at the time that was a terrible decision by the FA and still do. It was right over the top because the people in charge were not at the club when the rules were broken.'

With this passion on show, people were beginning to see Sugar as not just a businessman who worked in football, but as a football man who worked in business. Having suspected for years that he had no passion for the game at all, it seemed people were finally coming round.

Tony Berry, former chairman of the Blue Arrow employment services group, is a long-term ally of Sugar. It was from Berry that Sugar acquired 500,000 shares to gain the majority control of Tottenham. Berry insisted that his friend Sugar had become 100 per cent football. 'It is a major, major conversion. The whole family. When he got involved, he saw it as a business. I once said he saw it as 75 per cent business and 25 per cent sport. Now he's gone the whole way round. I've never seen such a transformation.'

Berry was clear on something else, too: that there was no way that Sugar was about to go the way of other club chairmen and ignore his business sense. 'This may be where the difference is. There's still that steel in him that will never let him forget what he's learned in business,' Berry claimed. 'I can tell you that all these moves have been made with the cash flow in mind and the Tottenham refinancing structure taken into account. Nothing is certain, of course, because we've seen other chairmen go the way. But he's the last man I'd expect to commit hara-kiri for the sake of football.'

Things were looking rosy in the White Hart Lane garden once more. However, just as quickly as the press leaped to hype up Klins-mania, so did they rush to throw water over it. Mick Dennis in the *Evening Standard* led the charge. Reporting on the German striker's enthusiasm, he wrote, 'Let us see if [Klinsmann] still feels that way after experiencing the North Circular on the way to spend a wet Wednesday evening mixing with Vinnie Jones and the rest of the Wimbledon Crazy Gang at Selhurst Park.' It was a typical insinuation thrown at foreign imports and a ridiculous one. Did Dennis really not believe that there were more than a few 'wet Wednesday evenings' in Germany? And there are tough opponents in every League. A player as decorated as Klinsmann would be more than familiar with that.

It would take several years for overseas players to begin to dispel this xenophobic attitude, and Klinsmann was central to this process, with a charm offensive on the British public in his early days in the Premiership. He even poked fun at his reputation for diving by incorporating a dive into his celebration of his first goal. The first people he won over were, of course, the Spurs faithful. 'People expecting a Nazi thug were disappointed,' said Stuart Mutler, former editor of club fanzine *Spur*. 'He seems friendly and open – not what you'd necessarily expect from a German. He's interested in the environment, drives a Beetle and likes back-packing. For goodness' sake, the man even smiles when he misses a chance at goal.'

Supporter Steve Davies echoed this impression: 'People like to pretend they've got certain prejudices, but, if we signed Ian Wright [of hated rivals Arsenal FC] and he scored lots of goals, everyone would like him. Psychologically, Klinsmann has turned the club around. He's brought a change in thinking. He doesn't just excite the fans, he excites the players. They've seen him on the telly and to be playing with him is a dream come true.'

The buoyancy Klinsmann had brought to the club was soon being compared to Frenchman Eric Cantona's impact at Manchester United – praise indeed! 'Foreign players are more sophisticated,' Davies insisted. 'They don't want to live in Cheshunt: they want to live in the centre of town. English players are stuck in a stereotypical laddish mould. If one admitted he went to an art exhibition, they'd call him a faggot.'

It seemed the German legend was transforming not just the club, but the culture of English football itself.

Rob Hughes, *The Times*'s influential football writer, gave Klinsmann a half-term report four months into the season. 'What more can we ask of Jürgen Klinsmann? He came to Britain a world-class star with a reputation, which he did not know he had, of being a dive who feigned claims for penalties. In half a season, he has charmed and

114

worked his way into our consciousness. We see him now as a decent man, a thundering good athlete and an honest performer. Speak to men who have refereed him and they use an old-fashioned term, a gentleman.' Hughes was decent enough to acknowledge, and indeed praise, Sugar's role in all this. 'It should be remembered that Alan Sugar's instincts were perfectly attuned to the game when he came off his yacht, *Louisiana*, in Monte Carlo to give a 2-million-pound handshake to a player who has quickly melted away British scepticism.' It appeared that Sugar was now earning praise from all quarters, having brought Jürgen to England.

Football legend Kevin Keegan added his voice the Jürgen love-in: 'I admire the way Klinsmann plays, with a smile on his face. Too many players look as if they are having a bad day at the office, they show the strain and the stress, but Jürgen smiles his way through and that's why the supporters have taken to him.'

Given Klinsmann's reputation as something of a cheat, it is significant that leading football referee Keith Cooper was also bowled over by the German striker. 'I have seen no evidence in this country of Jürgen Klinsmann diving during a match. During play, in which of course he speaks perfect English, I have to say I have found Klinsmann to be a model, a perfect gentleman.'

Klinsmann scored 21 goals in 41 appearances that campaign, and also collected the prestigious Football Writers' Association's Footballer of the Year award. He had been key in securing a respectable seventh-place finish for his club.

But then the bubble burst. Klinsmann quit White Hart Lane, saying that he was doing so in search of a club that had qualified for European football the following season.

Sugar was fuming: 'What total and utter rubbish!' he stormed. 'The danger is that people will believe the nonsense fed to them by Klinsmann and others. He came round to my house here, and we spoke for hours, hours and hours. We made every effort to keep him but we all know the real reason that he went. There are two Jürgen Klinsmanns. There is one who flashes those gleaming teeth for the cameras . . . that lovely smile . . . that butter wouldn't melt in the mouth. But in private there's another Jürgen Klinsmann, a hard-nosed businessman who knows what he wants.'

But Sugar admitted that the move seemed inevitable. 'Remember that Gary Lineker wrote an article within one month of the season starting in which he said Klinsmann would be leaving. He said Jürgen was being scouted by AC Milan and Bayern. I was angry with Gary at the time. But he was right and I got it wrong. I thought Klinsmann was a loyal guy and would stay for two years.'

Sugar was particularly angry that Jürgen had said that he was leaving in part because no money was available to strengthen the Tottenham team, and that key players had been allowed to leave. Not true, insisted Sugar. 'There was a board meeting back in May and it is minuted, that

Above: In April 1986, Sugar bought the rights to sell all Sir Clive Sinclair's computers in a world-wide deal worth £5 million.

Below: Another day, another massive deal – Rupert Murdoch and Alan Sugar come together over a model of the Astra satellite. Amstrad was to manufacture the dishes and receivers.

Above: Sugar and Terry Venables announce their takeover of Tottenham Hotspur in June 1991.

Below: Sugar with new signing Jurgen Klinsmann, who joined the club in the summer of 1994, and Ossie Ardiles.

Above: Gordon Brown MP in his first year as Chancellor with Alan Sugar to promote youth enterprise. The pair visited Sugar's old school of Hackney Community College.

Below: Chancellor Gordon Brown and Sir Alan meet young entrepreneurs in 2006.

Above: Sol Campbell lifts the Worthington Cup after Tottenham beat Leicester City 1–0 in March 1999.

Below: Alan Sugar and David Pleat at Tottenham.

On 13 June 2000, Sugar became Sir Alan at a Buckingham
Palace ceremony.

The Sugars attending *Best of the Empire* – a charity show at the Hackney Empire in East London. Sir Alan contributed to the redevelopment of the much-loved venue.

Sir Alan with Lord Mandelson, the former Secretary of State for Business, Innovation and Skills.

Doing what he does best – promoting entrepreneurship and business skills in the community.

we told our manager Gerry Francis that he had £7 million to spend. And, that was before we knew that Nicky Barmby was going. We fought day and night to keep Nicky Barmby.

'In fact, we signed him on a new four-year contract. I did that personally. But he just wanted to go. Everybody knows the reason why he wanted to live back up North. Every single penny of the Barmby money, plus more, is available for our manager to sign new players. Gerry's no mug. He specifically told me never to disclose how much we have to spend. He says it puts us in a bad position with people jacking up the price because they know how much we've got. But there is money sitting there waiting for the manager to spend it.'

Angry words, indeed, but there was worse to come. Sugar's interview on the subject on BBC's *Match of the Day* programme has become an iconic moment in football broadcasting history. 'Here's the last shirt he wore at the Leeds match,' said Sugar, showing the shirt to the camera. 'Look what he's written on there – "To Alan with a very special thank you." I'm bloody sure it's very special because I'm the bloomin' mug who relaunched his career. I wouldn't wash my car with this shirt now.

'You can give it to one of your viewers if you like, or auction it and give the money to some charity. Obviously an appropriate charity if we can. Something like a charity to get people to tell the truth in future or something like that.'

The more subdued club manager Gerry Francis added forlornly, 'Jürgen is irreplaceable.'

Maybe so, but Francis soon stabilised the club, and a great run at the end of the 1995/96 season saw them come within a whisker of European qualification.

However, the following season began badly for the club, with key players suffering from numerous injuries to and the team struggling at the wrong end of the Premiership table. Come November, Tottenham were languishing in 16th place of the 20-club Premier League, just one point off the relegation zone. Francis quit, citing 'personal pride' as the reason for his decision. 'Our results this season have not been good enough for me and certainly not good enough for Tottenham Hotspur Football Club,' he said at a news conference. 'You're judged by results and obviously the results weren't good enough.'

Sugar, appearing at Francis's side, said he had urged the manager to stay and blamed pressure from the media for forcing him out: 'Once again, I'm swallowing my principles in being forced to agree to do something which I know was not in the best interest of the club,' Sugar said. 'The credentials of the man are no different than when he first came here when everybody was singing his praises.'

Once again, it was time for a new manager, the fourth of Sugar's reign to date. The man he chose was not well known in English footballing circles, although the same was true of Arsène Wenger when he arrived in England the previous year, and he was now performing miracles at arch rivals Arsenal. So, had Sugar found Tottenham their own foreign genius? In a word, no.

When new boss Christian Gross was unveiled, it was clear that English football had a new character in its midst. At the press conference, he excitedly waved a London Underground train ticket at the cameras. 'I wanted to know the way the fans will come to White Hart Lane,' he said, to widespread amusement. 'I needed to show that I am one of them. This is a big, big job, a big, big challenge. I hope this is the ticket to my dream.' Sitting alongside a nodding Sugar, Gross added, 'I have to stop the fall. That means good team spirit, discipline inside and outside the team, and bringing in a new system.'

The smartly dressed Gross was clearly a disciplinarian. 'I was a team player,' he asserted. 'Teamwork was very important. For me there must be that spirit. If you have discipline, you are powerful. Players have to be disciplined.'

It had been a theatrical performance from the new manager, leaving most observers bemused at best, and one can only imagine what went through the players' minds.

However, even greater drama was about to unfold in north London, and nobody could have predicted the new twist in the plot. Football-supporting viewers of *GMTV* were no doubt aghast when Alan Sugar appeared on screen one morning in 1997 to announce that he had re-signed none other than Jürgen Klinsmann. During the interview with presenter Eamonn Holmes, a well-known Manchester United supporter, Sugar was asked about Spurs' visit to Old Trafford on 10 January. Sugar replied, 'I guess you expect you're going to get a few goals past us.' He then dropped the bombshell: 'But we've got Jürgen coming back. He's on a plane, he'll be landing in about half an hour's time and, subject to passing a quick medical this morning down at the local hospital in the city, we've got a press conference at 12.30. He's back to help us out for the rest of the season.'

Stunned doesn't begin to describe to the reaction of the football world. After a disappointing six months in Sampdoria, Klinsmann was back at White Hart Lane, thanks to the man who had publicly lambasted him when he quit.

However, it seemed Klinsmann was too busy smiling as ever to have any interest in raking over old ground: 'I feel now that I can give them a hand. I'll do all that I can for the team. I feel coming back here is a wonderful challenge. It's a bit like coming home. I'm very happy about it.'

It was an amazing shot in the arm for struggling Spurs, and the ultimate Christmas present for the Tottenham players and fans, who welcomed their hero back with open arms. As one senior player told the *Evening*

Standard, 'If Jürgen was just sitting in the stands it would lift the whole place.'

Sugar, too, seemed keen to let bygones be bygones, telling reporters, 'I think we had better push everything in the past behind us. He has seen we are in trouble and the opportunity has come up for him to help us out for a few months – and we have grabbed it.'

Once more, he had pulled a rabbit out of the hat. As Simon Greenberg concluded in the *Evening Standard*, 'It is to Sugar's credit though that he has allowed the reality of relegation to overcome his pride and for former feuds to be consigned to the scrapheap. With the decision to bring Klinsmann back, they will both take the accolades for saving Spurs' season.'

The German did indeed save the club's season, but, once more, come the end of the campaign, he was to leave the club under a cloud, although, this time, it was not as a result of a falling-out with Sugar, but with the manager Christian Gross. The German announced his plan to depart before the campaign was over.

Klinsmann said that he had been encouraged to take on a quasi-coach role within the dressing room, and that the manager had been less than enthusiastic about the advice he offered. 'When I came over, one thing Alan Sugar asked me for was my input and that is what I have done, telling Gross and the players what we should change and what we should do better,' he said. 'I have put a lot of energy doing that but I have had no feedback.

I have reached the point where I have to stop in order to concentrate on my own game.'

Unsurprisingly, iron man Gross was not overjoyed to be offered advice by one of his players. He retorted, 'I told Klinsmann that I am the man who makes the decisions. I am the man who decides where the players will play.' It seemed matters had come to a head after a match against Bolton Wanderers, as Gross confirmed: 'It is true that there was a row between Jürgen Klinsmann and myself after our win over Bolton. He was the only player not happy with what was a vital result and this was simply because he did not agree with where I had decided to play certain players and, in particular, David Ginola. I could not understand his reaction.'

Klinsmann bit back: 'Christian and I have totally different opinions about things and about handling things. But I just don't want any more of this stuff going on because we have enough problems with the relegation battle. At the end of the day, he is the manager and I respect that even if I do have different ideas. I have tried to give my input but it reached a certain point last week when our ideas differed. I will give my best until the end of the season and then we will go different directions.'

Gross had the final word. 'I have the greatest respect for what Jürgen has done in a long and successful international career,' said the Swiss head coach, 'but he is still a squad member and has to accept my decisions about who I play and where I play them.'

Tottenham survived the season with their place in the Premiership intact, but Klinsmann was once more on his way.

From one player who left, to another who never joined – and a moment that left a bitter taste in the mouth of Sugar, and of Tottenham's proud fans. The club had spent the best part of a year trying to tempt French midfield star Emmanuel Petit to sign for them. Having treated him to dinner on his private yacht, Sugar believed he had his man, and, after later showing the ponytailed Petit round the stadium, he lent him money for his taxi fare. An hour later, Sugar's mobile phone rang. It was Arsenal vice-chairman David Dein calling from his Totteridge home. 'You'll never guess who I've got here,' boasted Dein. 'Emmanuel Petit. We've just signed him.'

A fuming Sugar raged, 'I wouldn't mind so much, but I paid for his bloody taxi.'

Ah, well, you win some, you lose some. Petit confirmed this story in a newspaper column. 'Let me say, for the record, that it is all true, but that it gives me no pleasure to see Tottenham struggling after two disappointing results. I know there is a great rivalry between the two sets of supporters, but I was not born with that sense of antagonism.'

There is, indeed, no shortage of antagonism between Tottenham and Arsenal fans, so this story naturally became a legend in footballing circles, and became the subject of much banter between fans of the two north

London clubs. Arsenal fan Piers Morgan – then editor of the *Daily Mirror*, for which Sugar was to write a column – certainly took every chance he could to rib Sugar about it. 'I used to tease Sir Alan mercilessly about this when I was his boss and he always reacted extremely badly,' said Morgan.

Petit went on to be part of the Arsenal side that won the double in 1988, compounding the misery of the Tottenham folk. However, when he left the club three years later, Petit put the boot in on his former employers, calling them – ironically enough – 'apprentices'.

Another high-profile Arsenal signing that left Sugar somewhat red-faced was that of Dutch master Dennis Bergkamp. When Bergkamp signed for Arsenal in 1995, it seemed Sugar was still very much smarting from the first departure by Jürgen Klinsmann. He slammed Bergkamp's signing as 'cosmetic marketing' by Arsenal, and described foreign players such as Bergkamp somewhat bizarrely as 'Carlos Kickaballs' who would not prove a success. Eleven years later, laden with League and Cup-winning medals, Bergkamp left Arsenal, showing that Sugar had certainly been wide of the target on this occasion. Arsenal fans had the last laugh, although, to be fair to Sugar, plenty of other onlookers had been sceptical of the Dutchman when he first arrived in England, with Massimo Moratti, president of Inter Milan, saying, 'Arsenal will be lucky if Bergkamp scores ten goals this season.'

However, by this time, the two north London clubs had become the source of a far more spectacular story. Sugar was about to make one of his most audacious moves as Tottenham manager – and one he was in time to regret bitterly. Never before had the two rival clubs witnessed the like of what was about to happen. Scottish football legend George Graham is synonymous with Arsenal's history of success. As a player, he was a key part of the Gunners' side that won the 1971 double, and he returned to the club years later as manager, to guide them to a period of success that had not been seen since Herbert Chapman's legendary 1930s glory days. He won two League Championships, an FA Cup and League Cup, as well as conquering Europe with the 1994 Cup Winners' Cup victory over Italians Parma. During this period of sustained success for Arsenal, Graham had been the architect of numerous victories over Tottenham, as the Gunners utterly outclassed their rivals. Understandably, then, he was far from a popular figure among the White Hart Lane faithful.

So imagine their shock when they found out that their bitter enemy had been appointed manager of their club!

That was the incredible situation facing them in the autumn of 1998. At the press conference that saw Graham unveiled to a shocked public, Sugar was forthright in defending his move. Sitting alongside a tanned Graham, Sugar said, 'If you work for IBM or the Ford Motor Company, you would go for the best in the field, someone who has been successful. George is one of, if not the top manager in English football. Why has he come to Tottenham? Results, that's the end of it.'

It was a good sales pitch from a good salesman, and Graham's stock in English football was high at this time. However, Sugar knew that, thanks to the Scotsman's Arsenal associations, it would take a lot more than this to sell him to many of the White Hart Lane faithful. This was a courageous appointment indeed.

Giving the manager his unequivocal backing, Sugar asserted, 'The single most important man at a football club is the manager. Maybe we will start a trend here, but it should have happened a long time ago. We must never sit on the edge of our seats again wondering whether we will be relegated. If George is not successful, we should have to examine the reasons why. We will have to see if the place is doomed, I'm jinxed, or that we might have to get an exorcist in – or even [one-time England manager Glenn Hoddle's faith healer] Eileen Drewery. But the fact is we have not performed for the fans at all. We have not given them anything to cheer about. Some managers come in and wave chequebooks about and others get spontaneous results. George is consistently a winner and, in any walk of life, you have got to get those kind of people around you.'

It seemed Sugar had been taken aback by some of the flak that he taken from football fans during his short time in the game. He is no wimp, but, nonetheless, the ferocity of the abuse had stunned him and, for the first time, the prospect of quitting entered his vocabulary. 'I have passed my sell-by date in the eyes of the fans, but it's time to get this club in shape and performing well, give it the status it deserves. But there is a limit to the thickness of a rhino's skin and I won't put up with the abuse from the fans. It's just not worth it. However, I am in no frame of mind to think about selling out, it's as simple as that. But I like to work in an environment where there is a goal at the end of the rainbow or that your efforts are appreciated. The fans are part of our team here, and in appointing George I believe the board have made an excellent choice.

'Anything I do, in any companies that I own, you work as a team, and your efforts are appreciated. Having been branded cynical and a cold person who has no knowledge of football, or interest in the heritage and tradition of the club, you spend seven years trying to convince people it's not the case and in the end you go with the flow.'

Graham was similarly clear about what lay ahead. 'I just want people to be patient,' he told reporters. 'I have always been a manager involved in a building process wherever I have managed, like Millwall and Arsenal. Millwall fell to the bottom of the table before I got them promotion, and Arsenal could do no better than seventh before I got them success.'

And success was exactly what Graham brought to

Tottenham when he won the club their first trophy for eight years in the shape of the Worthington Cup. Facing the combative Leicester City in the final on 22 March 1999, Tottenham were heroes on the day. They played with just ten men for nearly half the game after seeing their defender Justin Edinburgh sent off. However, a poacher's goal from Dane Allan Nielsen was enough to win the day for them.

This was the club's first trophy under the Sugar reign, and he was delighted; he didn't even complain when captain Sol Campbell soaked him in champagne in the dressing room after the final whistle. There was acclaim from all quarters. David Pleat, director of football at Spurs, was gracious enough to praise the chairman, amid the celebrations. 'Now it's time for Alan to sit back and enjoy it. The chairman has gained experience from the first few years. Early on he had a few problems not of his making, as there was no one on the board with a football background.

'Very often mediocre players were signed. Very often cover was needed for injuries and sometimes players were bought on a whim simply as cover when they weren't really up to it. Now there is confidence in the management and I'm there to provide information and keep the chairman in touch. He is a hands-on chairman, and rightly so. He should be aware of everything that happens at his football club.'

As indeed he was, and Sugar would also have been

well aware that Tottenham's value on the stock market was back up close to £90 million and rising. He soon launched a new £5 million private jet, called the G-Spur, which was decked out in club colours. These were optimistic times at White Hart Lane. Could Spurs build on their Worthington Cup triumph to win one of the big trophies?

To do that, Graham would need more transfer funds, which he duly received. Sergei Rebrov had won eight League titles and four cups in nine years with Dynamo Kiev, scoring at a rate of almost a goal every game throughout his career, including 28 goals in 60 games in Europe. Winning 36 caps with Ukraine, Rebrov formed a deadly partnership with Andrei Shevchenko and even turned down a move to join his old partner at AC Milan in favour of a switch to White Hart Lane. But he didn't come cheap: his £11 million fee smashed the Tottenham transfer record. It had proved a painstaking process to sign Rebrov, and Sugar had bravely held out against the £12 million asking price.

But, finally, Spurs had their man and the manager was delighted. 'He is a quality player and a great acquisition,' Graham beamed. 'He is a team player and I have the philosophy individuals play, teams win Championships. He can play well with others but produce on his own as well, he is an ideal player for me.'

Although this was not quite a transfer in the Klinsmann mould, still, people seemed surprised that the

Ukrainian had chosen to come to White Hart Lane, and Rebrov was asked why he had turned down the mighty Milan in favour of Spurs. 'Maybe there would have been a better offer from Milan, but I dreamed of playing in England and the chairman and the club respected my wishes and so I am here,' he said. 'I know the team are going up and looking to win the English League and to be a part of that success would be a dream for me. I am confident about the future, I know the targets of the club. They told me they would like to bring more players in and I am very happy with that. Any club wanting to be the best must do that. I hope they will play in Europe very soon and I can help them to do that.'

However, Rebrov's magic was obviously not enough to lift Tottenham straight into title contention, and it seems George Graham would soon be knocking on Sugar's door wanting money for more players. 'I would like to think if I targeted someone I could buy him, but we are not there yet,' he said. 'If you look at the bench it's full of kids, but the youngsters we have bought are for the future.

'There is a lot of hard work to do here. I don't think you can challenge the top three for two or three years after avoiding relegation. The task of acquiring players to challenge is virtually impossible within that time. Right now the top of the League does not bother me. I've got to get us right and somewhere near that top six. The main problem we have had is long-term injuries. If I can get them back it will be a massive boost. But we still need new players. Without them I don't know how far we can go.'

By the time that fans' favourite David Ginola quit for Aston Villa, the writing seemed to be on the wall, as Sugar came under intense pressure to quit. And he eventually and uncharacteristically succumbed. 'No jokes. No tricks. I'm off. And I will do it in a professional manner,' he said. 'The company has made an announcement to the Stock Exchange that we are in talks with various people. As soon as any of these become statutory and reportable, we shall comment on them. There are no deals right now. But, as they say, we are hot to trot.' That trot came a step closer at the end of the year.

In December 2000, it was confirmed that leisure group ENIC, led by sports executive Daniel Levy, was buying 27 per cent of Tottenham chairman Sir Alan Sugar's majority stake in the club, giving it a total of 30 per cent. It was reported that this was the third time that Sugar had offered ENIC the chance to buy him out. Sugar would have been justified in allowing himself a wry chuckle when fans began more or less immediately to question ENIC's ambition. When it was revealed that ENIC believed it would take five years for them to turn the club's fortunes around, Bernie Kingsley, of the Tottenham Independent Supporters Association, said, 'If this means we are going to have to wait another five years before ENIC believes we're going to be major players again, the fans will not be happy. This is exactly the sort of thing we've heard year after year from Sugar. The fans want to see something happening soon. We want to know what ENIC's plans for the club are. We hope we're not going straight from the frying pan into the fire. We've already waited ten years for some sort of success.'

It appeared to be a case of new owners, but the same old story.

Sugar, meanwhile, seemed to be well out of it. He had stepped down as chairman, but not before winning a libel case against the *Daily Mail* for an article that unjustly branded him 'The Miser of N17'. He donated the proceeds of the case to the Great Ormond Street Hospital. Citing the personal abuse of his family as the straw that broke the camel's back, Sugar was relieved to be away from football. 'It is a sad end, mainly because I have been stuck with a label. They will talk about Alan Sugar as a money man and that's all down to people's attitude. But that's how I'll always be remembered.'

His position had become increasingly difficult, as the Spurs fans continued to turn on him. 'We want Sugar out!' became a depressingly familiar chant at White Hart Lane. Hunter Davies joked in the *Evening Standard*, 'The only solution for Sugar: Sack the Spurs fans and sign a new 10,000 crowd.'

However, the situation became far from amusing when details of a secret meeting of anti-Sugar Spurs 'supporters' was leaked to the media. A sinister three-point action plan was revealed:

'1. Boycott of goods such as programmes, drinks, etc. and of sponsors' goods like easyJet flights, Holsten beer – this would send the sponsors a signal there is a vote of no confidence in Sugar.
2. Demonstrate at every home game, win or lose, to embarrass Sugar.
3. Abuse his family.'

In addition, an anti-Sugar website, with his mobile phone number on it, was published on the Internet. No wonder Sugar, a man who has always put family well before business, had had enough.

After leaving Tottenham, Sugar seemed to remain bitter about much of what went on there, and took a swipe at George Graham, after the Scotsman had blamed Sugar for the club's continued woes. 'George Graham is very experienced at playing the media game, orchestrating the press with a clever quote or an easy headline. Unfortunately, many fans can't see through this little trick unless someone like me spells it out,' wrote Sugar. 'But let me ask you something: Have you ever noticed nothing is ever George Graham's fault? And I mean nothing. Now how can that be true? None of us are perfect, yet George has cleverly mastered the art of deflection and is very successful at diverting attention from himself and his failings.' He joked that, even if footage was found of George Graham robbing a bank, it would be blamed on Alan Sugar and not the Scotsman. He concluded, 'In my time at Tottenham I made lots of mistakes, the biggest was possibly employing him.'

Looking back over his up-and-down reign at White Hart Lane, Sugar was philosophical but blunt. 'What went wrong was, I think, my persistence in thinking that perhaps I could make it a successful business and also successful on the football pitch,' he said. 'What went wrong is my poor reading of the situation. After year in, year out trying to do things that way, what went wrong was it took me too long to realise that I was pissing in the wind, literally wasting my time, banging my head up against the wall. That's what went wrong. My fault.' Having accepted his part of the responsibility – a very Alan Sugar trait – he fired a defiant parting shot at football, and looked to the future. 'It was a waste of my life. I think a clever person, a clever outside observer who wants to do a commercial analysis on me, should track Amstrad's results throughout the course of that ten years, then track them now. After I leave Tottenham and get back to concentrating on Amstrad, you start to see the profits rising again. And that tells a story. No one's picked up on that really. The story is, I suppose, I'm a one-horse pony man, or whatever you want to call it. When I give my attention to something I tend to give it all and I think, in hindsight, that, apart from my losing ten years out of my life, Amstrad shareholders actually lost me for a while. I took my eye off the ball for a wasted, hopeless, ungrateful bunch of people.'

'You could forgive Alan Sugar for renaming Tottenham's ground White Hart Strain after his troubled tenure as Spurs chairman,' commented Peter Sanderson on the BBC website.

And perhaps he thought ENIC should take that strain, as he moved, onwards and upwards, to his next challenge – and his next moment of glory.

CHAPTER SEVEN
ARISE, SIR ALAN SUGAR

The New Year's honours list announced on 31 December 1999 had a special edge to it, as it was the Millennium year. Among those announced on the list were Sir Sean Connery, Dame Elizabeth Taylor, Dame Shirley Bassey, Dame Julie Andrews, Henry Cooper, Stirling Moss, Richard Branson and Norman Wisdom. These were hallowed shoulders to be rubbing on such a prestigious list, and an honour for Alan Sugar, the working-class boy from Hackney made good, to be included in this list. Indeed, it was a special list in another way too. The Prime Minister's spokesman Alastair Campbell explained that many of those nominated fell into the category of being an 'icon', among which he included Alan Sugar.

Sugar was overjoyed and somewhat amused to learn of this news. 'I'm tickled pink,' he told reporters. He then explained that he felt the significance of this news went far beyond the personal. 'It is a great honour and a wonderful sign of the times that a man that started his life in a working-class background should, through hard work and application, be honoured by his country. Young people should take this as a signal that in Britain today anything is possible if the will to succeed is strong enough.' However, the moment of joy was tinged with a little sadness. 'My only regret is that my mum and dad are no longer here to enjoy this moment,' said the man shortly to become Sir Alan Sugar.

The response from the media was supportive. In modern times, an element of cynicism about knighthoods and other honours has crept into public discourse. However, it was generally agreed that the man who began in business by selling car aerials out of his boot and rose to become a multimillionaire was about as suitable a recipient for such an honour as it was possible to imagine. And even the mischievous lot over at the *Daily Mirror*'s 'City Slickers' finance column offered their congratulations to both Sugar and Branson. 'Congratulations to our good pals Alan Sugar and Richard Branson on their long overdue knighthoods,' they wrote. 'What do we call you guys now? Sir, Sir Al, Sir Dickie? Let us know mateys.' A few days later they followed up, cheekily claiming that a rise in Amstrad's share value was in part down to them. 'The City is going crazy over Sir Alan Sugar's Amstrad, after we made it our top tip for 2000. The shares have already jumped 48 per cent so far this year to 311p. More to the point, our tip has helped make Sugar £22.3 million since the turn of the century. You know where to find us, Sir Al, and if you want our bank account details, just ask.'

Six months later, the Amstrad boss officially became Sir Alan Sugar at Buckingham Palace. He was only permitted three guests on the day, after a bit of family deliberation, he chose to take his wife Ann, daughter Louise and son Daniel.

'I was only allowed three guests so the kids had to fight over it. But they managed to arrive at a peaceful arrangement.' He describes the moment when he was knighted by the Queen on 13 June 2000, as 'one of the proudest moments of my life'.

This phrase gives us a telling insight into his mind and priorities. Some men, on receiving a knighthood, will have regarded it as *the* proudest moment of their life. The man who built a business empire from scratch will have a host of proud moments during his working life, and, in his personal life, where marrying Ann and becoming a father and grandfather will also have been milestone moments. Although Sugar did not elaborate about the other proud moments that stand alongside his knighthood, it's a safe bet to assume such precious family moments will have been at the top of the pile.

But he was naturally full of pride and joy at his knighthood. Beaming, he said, 'It was a great day, a wonderful occasion. I seem to have come a long way and that is a great, great feeling. It shows how someone can start from a humble background and go on to be very successful. It shows the country that anything is possible. These honours certainly help break down the class barriers.'

It is typical of him to see the wider picture and to use his proud moment to offer hope and encouragement to others from his background.

As to how his relatives felt about his knighthood, he managed to express their pride but also maintain a refreshing slice of that Sugar gruffness, which none of his admirers would ever want him to lose. 'I don't think there were any tears shed but I know they were certainly very proud of me,' he said. 'It is just wonderful to get some recognition.'

As for the monarchy itself, Sir Alan showed a deep-felt appreciation of the institution. He said of the royal family, 'They are something the whole world takes the mickey out of but actually they are fantastic – and really should be kept. We must start to appreciate that and leave them alone.'

Others to be honoured on the day included *Auf Wiedersehen Pet* actor Timothy Spall, who had fought leukaemia for four years, who received an OBE. He had flown in specially from America for the event. 'They would only let me come back to the UK to come to this, otherwise I would still be working,' he said, smiling. Actress Alison

Steadman of *Singing Detective* and *Abigail's Party* fame was also made an OBE and said, 'I am absolutely thrilled, it is a great honour to be here.'

When Sugar was called forward for his knighthood, the announcer mentioned that the honour was being bestowed upon him for his work with computers and electronics. However, when he presented himself to the Queen, she told him that everyone would actually know him as a result of his involvement in football. Speaking of his work in the beautiful game, she said to Sir Alan that it must be a 'a rather precarious business'.

Sugar smiled knowingly and replied, 'Yes, it certainly is.'

So, would Sir Alan let his knighthood go to his head? Of course not, as he immediately showed after the event. As he spoke to reporters, he quickly turned the subject from his knighthood to the previous evening's football match.

It had been a dramatic game, which saw Portugal come back from two goals down to defeat England in the first-round tie of the European Championships. 'It was very disappointing,' he said. 'I really thought in the first fifteen minutes that we were going to win. But we are still in with a chance.' A lot of men would have been too distracted the evening before a knighthood to watch football, and many would have been too excited after a knighthood to even think about the previous evening's match. Not Sir Alan, who remained as down to earth as ever in the face of his newfound status. (It should also have shown those who, during his Tottenham Hotspur era, claimed that Sugar did not care about the game that they were clearly wrong.)

Cynics sometimes point to the fact that everyone has to use the 'Sir' prefix while addressing Sugar on *The Apprentice* and suggested that it is somehow bigheaded of him to insist on this. However, read any interview with Sugar since his knighthood and you will struggle to find any significant mentions of the knighthood, or his memories of his day at Buckingham Palace. While he has accepted the honour with joy and grace, he has also moved on, to write the next chapter of his life, a chapter that has included further honours. The man that left school at 17 with a mixed attitude, having been interested in part in furthering his education, was made an honorary doctor of science by City University, in recognition of his close involvement with the business school, including establishing the Amstrad Research Scholarship. He received his degree from Professor Andrew Chambers, the dean, at a ceremony at London's Guildhall.

Five years later, he added another honorary degree to his collection, when Brunel University also made him an honorary doctor of science. He received the award on 12 July at Wembley Conference Centre. 'I am delighted to accept this degree from a famous university that specialises in technology, a field that has been close to my heart all of my professional life. It is a great honour they felt my contribution to technology over the years has warranted this.'

'You don't need a degree to be great,' said an opinion piece in the *Daily Express* on 19 August 2005. It went on to praise Sugar for making it big in business without a university education. 'Sir Alan Sugar, the multimillionaire who started electronics company Amstrad and stars on TV, never dreamed of Oxford. His higher education took place at a market stall.'

It was nice that the article praised Sugar this way, but, by the time this article was published, it was not technically correct, as Sir Alan actually had two degrees.

Later that year, Sugar returned to give Brunel students a lecture. The evening, sponsored by HSBC Bank, took the form of 'An Evening with Sir Alan'. 'I enjoy being accessible, recognisable and perhaps a role model for the public,' he said, looking forward to the event. 'It's equally important to be able to have a rapport with a live audience. I'm looking forward to being in the hot seat myself for a change.'

It turned into an enjoyable and memorable evening. Sugar had been key in orchestrating the evening's schedule. He dismissed the idea of simply giving a lecture, because he finds speeches – both giving them and listening to them – boring. Brunel vice-chancellor Professor Steven Schwartz, introducing Sugar, said, 'It's a Q&A session and nothing is really off-limits. If it is, I'm sure Sir Alan will let you know!'

As it turned out, nobody asked anything that he was not absolutely delighted to answer.

Joseph Baines, the president of the Union of Brunel Students, asked the first question: 'Why do you think that nationally we are struggling to excite youngsters into a career in engineering? And how would you go about promoting engineering as a profession to the youth of today?'

Sugar replied, 'Engineers are underpaid and under-valued in this country. Engineering needs to be made more attractive – at the moment people want to become consultants, as it is an easy route to put money in their pockets. In countries such as France, engineers are regarded much more highly, in the same bracket as doctors and lawyers.'

Later in the evening, Lady Kitty Chisholm, Brunel's director of development, asked Sugar about his well-known dislike of schmoozing. He must have done some of it himself, though, she suggested.

'I was told in my younger days that "this is what you do", so I did wine and dine – it was dull and insincere,' replied Sugar. 'Younger people have to do it for me now as I don't have the patience! Entertaining is now a big industry. It drives things like corporate hospitality at race days and football. It is now a deliberately prepared corporate expense. That's how it is in business, people are used to the jollies. Take them away and people might leave.'

He also ventured that it was vital for the future of business in the UK that a business culture be instilled in children from an early age. When one student queried whether there might turn out to be negative consequences if too much business culture was allowed into the classroom, Sir Alan snapped, 'I'm sick and tired of the "goody-goody" atmosphere in this country. I can see a court case coming from this question: you've stressed my child and I'm going to sue.'

This brought the discussion neatly round to Sugar's own educational experience, and he was asked, 'Are you now sorry that you did not stay on at school and possibly go to university?'

'The honest answer is no – in my case I'm brighter than most of the students here,' he quipped. 'It's a different era now, though. I'm often asked the question when I talk to students in schools, "Do qualifications matter?" And the answer to that is yes. The HR manager doing the recruiting can't see your personality, so if the qualifications aren't on your CV it goes in the bin. That might be unfair, but it's the harsh reality. You need to get qualifications, otherwise you'll be in the bin. You've got to have qualifications in order to achieve – it's the way into your first job. In fact, staying on might have hindered me. I started my own company at 17; if I'd been in school I might have gone on to do a gap year or something and wasted even more time!'

Instead, he has kept moving onwards and upwards. In

fact, quite literally upwards, for Alan Sugar has long enjoyed the delights of air travel. Whether as a pilot, or as a passenger in a private jet, he cherishes his time in the sky. There are no nagging phone calls, no emails, no disturbances. Perhaps it was during one of these journeys that he saw a gap in the private-jet travel market? He then launched a new company – Amsair, once more using an acronym of his initials to name the company. It seems he was ready to see his business instincts quite literally reach for the skies.

Amsair for a long while was managed by Sugar's son Daniel, who proved his business acumen by making it a major success story. He had been ushered into the family business very early in his life, and he took no time in showing that his father's faith in him was utterly justified. Daniel left school at 16 and went straight to work in the marketing department of Amstrad. It was a memorable first day for the teenage boy. His father took him to see Thomas Power, the head of marketing, and barked, 'This is Daniel. This is my son. I want you to teach him all that marketing crap you lot go on about down here. I want you to teach him everything you know. If he gives you any talkback, send him up to me. And, if he doesn't do what you tell him, throw him out the door.'

Power was very quickly impressed with young Daniel. 'He's got the bolshy, "Oh yeah, I'm a trader, I'm a banana salesman, and I'll sell you a satellite dish on the side" attitude,' said the marketing manager admiringly.

And so on to the Amsair project. The thinking behind Amsair was simple enough. Many rich, successful and famous people live the dream of travelling via private jet. As we have seen, Sugar has been known to fly by private jets often, and even to fly them himself on occasion. It might seem flash, but who, in his shoes, wouldn't fancy a bit of private travel? However, Sugar has gone one better by starting his own private-jet charter company. That way, he can feed his own love of private jets, by making money out of them.

Amsair Executive Aviation was formed in 1993, and is used by pop stars and businesspeople for their exclusive travel. An international aircraft charter company, it provides private-jet charter across the globe, with an extensive range of private jets, which includes the UK's largest owned fleet of Cessna Citation Excel aircraft. The firm's private-jet charter fleet is split into four sections: Turbo Prop Aircraft, Entry Level Private Jets, Mid-Size Business Jets and Heavy Aircraft. Technical details aside, the project can be summed up as: if you've got the money, they've got the jets.

However, the flights themselves represent only one aspect of what Amsair can offer their clients. They also offer executive jet charter consultancy and air charter concierge services. As Amsair's literature proudly boasts, they believe their customers deserve the best private jets available, which is why their aircraft charter department steps in the moment you book your trip and accommodates your every need. It is all part of the glorious Amsair experience. The attraction of all this to the wealthy is obvious. As anyone who has travelled in the air in recent times will know, it is a form of transport fraught with stresses and irritants; everything about air travel seems to have become more difficult and more perilous. Firms such as Amsair are perfectly positioned to cash in on this discontent. 'No more long queues at airports, no more security worries,' reads the proud blurb on the company website. 'A private jet for just you and your guests. You fly from your chosen airport to your chosen destination at a time that suits you! You depart from a beautiful private lounge away from all the hustle and bustle, where you can be sipping champagne waiting to board one of our luxury private jets.' No wonder they have so many people queuing up to use their services.

Daniel Sugar oversaw the development of the many services that Amsair offers clients. 'We are set up rather differently from most private-jet companies,' he explained. 'The aircraft are brand new. We offer pretty much a concierge service for private clients. We look after every detail from the moment a client has booked.' This is no small detail, but rather a fundamental selling point for Amsair, which distinguishes it from much of the competition. Food is just one example of how Amsair can personally tally their service to what clients demand, as Daniel Sugar explains. 'Clients may want a meal ordered from somewhere else, and we'll organise that. We'll also be flight-tracking to check for any possible delays and we'll triple-check the car transfers at either end of the journey.' Anyone who has had the dubious pleasure of standard airlines' catering will immediately grasp both the significance and appeal of services such as this. Likewise, those who have arrived at a new destination exhausted from a long flight only to find that the car they had arranged to get them to their hotel has fallen through will see the attraction of a company that so thoroughly checks arrangements.

It is for these, as well as other reasons, Daniel argues, that Amsair truly stands out thanks to its method of operating, and the range of services it offers. 'It's the attention to detail that gives someone the leading edge. Rather than being price-led, the big corporates prefer to use us because we get the service right. Our tailor-made package is really a bit different to our competitors.'

Their fleet of Cessnas is used to ferry British business chiefs to their meetings. 'We want to cut out the middleman and tell them if you charter our plane we will guarantee an excellent service at an excellent price,' said Daniel.

It is a company that has captured the imagination of the aviation industry. 'Start-up Amsair eyes gap in business market', announced the *Flight International* trade paper at launch. Daniel Sugar told the journal, 'There is a gap in the market for high-quality transatlantic business travel.'

In August 2004, they encountered a noticeable jump in business, and were delighted that their Citation Excel planes were 25 per cent busier than in the previous month. There was more good news the following month when their new Raytheon Premier One charter aircraft received its full certification for public charter. This was no small technical detail, as it actually opened up a whole new set of business opportunities for Amsair. Spokesman Philip Cartwright was delighted at this development: 'This plane offers a larger cabin than almost every entry-level jet and together with its unrivalled in-flight performance it allows our clients to get from A to B quicker, more comfortably and more economically than if they used other entry jets. Being that it's the only Premier 1 in the UK for public charter, the demand for this particular aircraft is very high.' They based the new fleet at Luton Airport, just north of London.

In November 2004, the Amsair fleet swelled again. Complete with 13 double club seats, two beds, screens and DVD players, the Embraer Legacy business jet was a fantastic option for long-term travel. As Daniel Sugar said, 'We are really excited about this plane; we see that this aircraft will be a workhorse for some of our VIP clients in the entertainment and showbiz industries as well as corporate executives.' Within weeks, the Embraer Legacy became the first jet of its kind to be fully certified for steep approach landings at London City Airport (LCY). This was highly significant, as Daniel explained,

'I think it's going to make a huge difference; in fact, we've had quite a few charters already out of LCY, and the charter order book is already looking very encouraging for clients based around that area. It's very convenient for clients based near by who want to fly long-range in significant comfort. Ours was the first Legacy to be approved for LCY. It's a huge benefit, not only for London City, but for short runways in general.'

All in all, 2004 had been a great year for Amsair, with an increase in turnover, profit and fleet size, and they opened a new office in Vienna, Austria. In 2005, the company went a step further and opened a branch in America, which was located in Boca Raton, Florida. As a proud Daniel Sugar put it, 'The opening of our US office will give our client base even greater flexibility and will allow Amsair to further enhance its existing client base within the American marketplace.'

Meanwhile, the Embraer Legacy jet had proved such a success with Amsair clients that the company bought a third plane. 'It is a superb aircraft and clients have really taken to it,' said a jubilant Daniel Sugar. Soon, this jet was included in the United States Visa Waiver Program, which made life much easier for everyone.

Make no mistake, all this is more than just hype. You can really judge the success of a company on how satisfied its customers are, and Amsair boasts plenty of satisfied clients. One such person was Michele Melliger, a 24-year-old graduate who wrote an article for the *Daily Mail*'s

'Femail' section about luxury air travel. For Christmas, Melliger's mother had bought her a luxury trip to Paris, including travel by private jet courtesy of Amsair. 'I could barely catch my breath as I opened the envelope my mum handed to me two weeks before Christmas last year,' wrote lucky Michele. 'In it were two tickets for a weekend in Paris flying by private jet and staying at the £600-a-night George V Hotel close to the Champs Elysées. Mum has always been generous at Christmas, giving me designer clothes, diamond jewellery costing upwards of £2,000 a piece, plus holidays to Miami and the Bahamas. But this was the ultimate present.'

Having encountered private air travel, Michele and her mother concluded 'that there's really nothing to rival flying by private jet'.

It was quite an experience for the pair. It started in a plush lounge at London City Airport, where they had to wait only minutes before being escorted to their private jet. Her mother had paid just under £15,000 to hire a six-seater plane from Amsair. Michele noted admiringly that there would be plenty of room for them to put their shopping on the return flight. As they settled into the plane, they sank into the cream leather seats, kicked off their shoes and curled their toes in the deep-pile carpet. They were served Moët & Chandon bubbly and canapés on takeoff. After a blissful weekend in Paris, shopping in the French capital's many designer boutiques, they flew home, again courtesy of Amsair. 'When it was time to fly home on the Sunday, we arrived at the private airfield just outside Paris around ten minutes before we were due to take off,' gushed Michele. 'This was definitely the beauty of flying in style – you skip all the dreadful waiting of normal air travel. Once again we were greeted with champagne and canapés, rounding off the most amazing Christmas gift.'

Other satisfied customers are queuing up to offer positive testimonials of their Amsair experience. The chief executive of the Multi National Electronics Corporation said, 'Amsair provide a service of the highest level. Their flexibility, dedication and ability to meet any schedule has been invaluable to the growth of our European business.' Pop stars and music industry chiefs have been loyal customers of Amsair, and the chairman of the US Music Group summed up the feelings of many customers when he said, 'In our industry we rely on service, reliability and flexibility. Amsair have constantly delivered all three of the above. When we place our clients on an Amsair plane, we can relax.'

The CEO of Worldwide JET Charter Broker added, 'Amsair is absolutely essential to our everyday business, whether it is a charter flight to or from London, Moscow or the Middle East. Amsair accommodate all our requests with the utmost attention to detail, they offer the ultimate in quality, reliability and professionalism. It is a pleasure having a working relationship with the team at Amsair.'

Having offered private jets to wealthy clients who travel to sporting events such as World Cup 2006 in Germany – this was probably as close as Sir Alan wanted to get to football after his 'White Hart Strain' experiences – the company had a gaming tie-in of a different kind in September 2008, when Amsair was named as the official airline of the World Series of Poker Europe. The deal was a great coup for Amsair, and it allowed Betfair Poker customers exclusive and discounted rates on any of the private jets in the extensive Amsair charter fleet. Philip Cartwright, Amsair's executive aviation sales director, expressed the firm's delight at this deal. 'We are constantly looking at new opportunities and ways to expand the business,' he said. 'The poker community is one of the fastest growing and affluent in the world. It makes sense for our two companies to be aligned and offer our services to the High Rollers at Betfair.'

The head of Betfair Poker, Bruce Stubbs, was equally overjoyed. 'We are delighted to have concluded this deal with Amsair,' he said, beaming. 'Betfair Poker are happy to provide a unique experience to our customers and what better way than to arrive at the largest and most prestigious poker event in Europe on an private jet provided by Amsair.'

However, for the majority of us, most of our knowledge of Amsair comes from one of the tasks in the second series of *The Apprentice*, when the contestants had to produce a television advertisement for the business – a neat way of bringing the company's existence to the attention of millions of television viewers without having to pay for advertising, and without subverting any broadcasting rules.

But, inevitably, the fact that Amsair is run by Sugar's son Daniel has rankled with some sour observers, as evidenced in the 'City Spy' column in the *Evening Standard*, which reported, 'The product they advertise is a booking card for Amsair, Sugar's executive jet business. It is run by his son, Daniel, who makes his debut on the programme. What's that? You thought Sir Alan was a tough-minded meritocrat?'

It seems the connection between Amsair and *The Apprentice* could have continued beyond the show's airing. After the second series finished, Sugar offered one of the contestants, Paul Torrisi, a job on the show. 'Yes, Sir Alan called me down to London and, yes, he offered me a job,' said Torrisi. The runner-up continued, 'Immediately after the programme had finished, Alan Sugar rang and asked if I'd come to London to meet his son Daniel. They wanted me to work at Amsair but I decided not to. I also got a call from a fund company offering me £4 million for my property portfolio. I thought, I'll take that, thank you.'

Torrisi went on to explain that Sugar's proposition had come on a particularly significant day for him. 'Coincidentally, it was the same day my wife gave birth. He wanted me to work for his private-jet company Amsair, but he said, "Paul, you're probably going to be inundated with offers and maybe you should come back to me in one or two years' time."' So it seems the pair went their separate ways.

As did Amsair and one of its best-known and more controversial clients, Richard Desmond, the extremely wealthy British publisher, owner of *Express* newspapers, and founder of Northern & Shell, which publishes *OK!* and *Star* magazines.

Despite his huge personal fortune, estimated as being at around the £550 million mark, when Desmond flew using the Amsair jets, he reportedly still tried to cut himself a special deal to receive a discounted rate for his flights with the company. But it seems he was given short shrift, as Sir Alan revealed in April 2007. 'Desmond doesn't use Amsair any more 'cos he's a *schnorer*,' he snapped.

The *Daily Express* slammed a series of *The Apprentice* as '*Big Brother* on wheels' under the headline 'Sugar's Bitter taste of failure'. Sugar was unmoved.

'His coverage of the current series is pathetic,' he said.

These clashes aside, Amsair continued to soar. With the much-publicised credit crunch of 2008, one might think that luxuries such as private jets would have been the first cutback as people and businesses very much tightened their belts. As banks massively reduced their lending to each other because they were uncertain about how much money they had, the result was more expensive loans and mortgages for ordinary people. A more noticeable result, though, was a general air of financial uncertainty from the man and woman on the street to the millionaire in the boardroom. Daniel Sugar acknowledged that Amsair was aware of this, and was ready to cope it. 'We are mindful of the fact that the economy isn't marvellous at the moment and, as it's a competitive industry, we can't be too expensive. We are not going after huge turnover. We have long-standing clients – about 60 to 70 of them – but they come back to us because we don't let them down. We run a lean machine and are clear in what we offer.' That lean machine continues to offer a great service, and looks set to climb to even greater heights in the future.

Just as Sir Alan enjoys the benefits of private air travel as both a businessman and customer, he also likes to travel in style on the road. It is the dream of many aspiring millionaires to own that most prestigious of cars and traditional symbol of wealth, the Rolls-Royce. As a man who has worked hard and cleverly, in order to amass a huge fortune, Sir Alan has treated himself to a taste of the Rolls-Royce experience. His most famous 'Roller' down the years was the Rolls-Royce Phantom. The car almost became a celebrity in its own right, thanks to the memorable footage of it when it first appeared as his mobile office in the second series of *The Apprentice*, replacing the 1998 Rolls-Royce Silver Seraph of the first series of the hit reality show. As motoring magazine *Autotrader* puts it, 'They don't come more luxurious than his old Rolls-Royce Phantom, a Goodwood-built four-door saloon powered by a 6.7-litre V12 engine producing 453bhp and a titanic 531lb/ft of pulling power. This engine accelerates the 2.5-ton prestige car from 0–62mph (100kph) in just 5.9 seconds and on to a limited top speed of 149mph.'

As well as these impressive technical specifications, the experience of actually being driven in such a car is a joy. Rear-seat passengers – and many owners will be chauffeur-driven rear-seat passengers – enjoy a near-silent travelling environment and the electronically controlled air suspension remains wonderfully composed. Little wonder, then, that, in 2006, the car beat off challenges from Daimler, Bentley and Mercedes for the *Autocar* title of best car. *Autocar*'s Rob Aherne said it won on merit, stating, 'This is a hard-earned and significant award for Rolls-Royce and British workmanship. It's been a good 50 years since a Rolls-Royce could honestly be described as best in the world.'

The car has become so associated with Sir Alan that news of the *Autocar* gong was immediately connected to him in the eyes of the press. The *Sun*'s headline was typical: 'Sugar's car is sweetest motor'.

Thanks to this association, interest in the car has rocketed in recent years, and not just in the motorcar trade press and tabloid newspapers. *The Times* sent motoring expert and all-round celebrity Jeremy Clarkson to test-drive the latest model. Having been initially sceptical, Clarkson was soon won over. 'The new Phantom is supposed to be the last word in engineering excellence, a road-going private jet, a luxury yacht with a point, a car that separates and distances you from both the tedium and the discomfort of travel.

'Ever wondered what it would be like to drive around in Salisbury Cathedral?' he asked his readers, with typically Clarkson-esque flourish. 'Well, you need wonder no more.' After painting such a gentle picture of the Phantom, he then turned to its more robust side, deploying more ebullient imagery that Sir Alan no doubt will have enjoyed. 'This one looks like it might kick your head in, for fun,' roared an admiring Clarkson.

The controversial pundit was absolutely blown away by the Phantom. His closing remarks give yet more insight into how the experience of the car would feel from the rear-seat perspective of Sir Alan Sugar. 'I am in no doubt that this is the best-engineered car ever made. It does not blind you with gadgets or boggle your mind with speed. It is supremely comfortable, but you can still sense what the front tyres are doing, even from the passenger seat. It is utterly and fabulously exquisite and I have no hesitation in giving it five stars.'

But, having given it five stars himself down the years, Sir Alan parted company with the Phantom in June 2008 when he put it up for sale with an asking price of £179,000, although without his famous 'AMS1' number plate, which he kept for his new car. Richard Johnson, sales manager at Sytner Rolls-Royce dealership in Knutsford, Cheshire, where the car was being sold, said that interest was huge and fast. 'We've already had a massive amount of interest,' he said within days of the car going up for sale. 'I don't think it will hang around long.'

Sugar was replacing his original Phantom model with the new long-wheelbase Rolls-Royce Phantom, which was to set him back hundreds of thousands of pounds. What a far cry from the days when he bought his first ever car, a minivan, for £50 back in 1967! Who could have dreamed back then that he could go on to make such riches, and to be able to buy such prestigious luxurious cars as these?

Sir Alan's riches have come through the sort of hard work and dedication to excellence that has been the hallmark of the Rolls-Royce company throughout its equally prestigious history. True, his career has not always run as smoothly as the Rolls-Royce experience promises. But he has kept moving forward, and has done so with the sort of quietly roaring determination that is the hallmark of the finest motorcars of the world offer. And, although he is now in his sixties, his ambition and enthusiasm know no bounds.

One of Alan Sugar's lesser-known side projects is Amsprop, his real-estate vehicle. Formed in 1985, it had as its first significant purchase a high-street parade in Barkingside, Essex. It grew and grew alongside Sir Alan's love of the property market and the company now owns an estimated half a billion pounds' worth of property. Sugar got a real thrill from the property world because there are few things in business he enjoys more than closing deals, and property allowed him plenty of chances to do just that. He was impulsive about it, and colleagues would often be told to close a deal within an hour to buy buildings worth millions of pounds that Sugar had not even personally visited. 'Everybody has a good laugh at me, because they cannot believe the way I go about doing property deals. I buy and sell properties without even going to look at them,' he said back then. His approach was also governed by a basic rule that he would not bother with any property worth less than £2 million. It's all right for some!

Amsprop was a family affair from the start. Sugar first employed his brother Derek, and then his son Daniel. After focusing mainly on regional property, the company eventually began to invest in larger West End real estate. 'Amstrad was booming away and I said this is my gambling business,' said Sugar. 'Why not break it off and start investing?'

He turned to his friend Ivor Spiro and Essex estate agent Douglas Allen Spiro, who suggested Sugar should purchase property at auction. The first deal he did that way was to buy a property in Basildon. 'It was one of the earliest and best deals I have done. I said to my son the other day, 'I could do with another 500 of those,' said Sugar. Amsprop was on the up.

In 1995, he bought Gloucester House – which includes London's Hard Rock Café – in Park Lane for £13 million. (Seven years later he sold just one of the penthouses within it for a cool £7 million.) However, even this shrewd purchase was outdone in terms of iconic stature by his big deal of the following year. In September 1996, he bought the IBM building on London's South Bank. The building, which sits next to the National Theatre, was sold by UK European Investments, controlled by the Lewis Trust Group, better known as the owner of the River Island fashion chain. By the turn of the century, there could be no doubt that Amsprop really began to mean business. Reportedly, Sugar was hit with a massive capital-gains tax bill from the sale of his stake in Tottenham Hotspur and opted to invest in West End property in the hope that the rise in capital values would help pay the taxman. He began to splash out on corner buildings in London, where retail rents on the ground floor are higher. These included Albemarle House on the corner of Grafton Street just off New Bond Street, Sackville House at 40 Piccadilly on the corner of Sackville Street, and Bennet House at 54 St James's Street by the Ritz hotel. Amsprop soon established a core estate in and around Mayfair and St James's, spending tens of millions of pounds there. As Daniel Sugar, an Amsprop director, said, 'Mayfair is still the prime location for retailers and office occupiers and we continue to strengthen our portfolio with the right opportunities.'

Looking back over the rise and rise of Amsprop, Sugar made it all sound rather easy. 'Gambling with electronics generated spare cash, which I flung into real estate,' he said. 'We've been in this position for ten years, with loadsa money in loadsa property. We entered this market to be safe with flagship buildings and reliable covenants. That's what we did, but now we're happy to gamble. We've got cash and our buildings and we'll let the grass grow under our feet if we don't do something with it. Our main focus now will be to become a traditional property company. We'll be buying investments and working them hard, possibly breaking them up and trading them on. It's time to get more involved.'

He was soon adding to the team and the portfolio. 'Daniel has been managing the existing portfolio for the past six or seven years. I'm not undermining that. He has picked up a lot of the tricks of the trade and knows the Mayfair market and Mayfair traders and agents or villains – or whatever you call them – very well, but we are ready to broaden our horizons into dealing and development. We're open for business. There's no deal that would be too big for us to handle.'

In 2008, Amsprop paid Scottish Widows £31.25 million for a prime corner freehold at 291 Oxford Street and Harewood Place, London W1. Daniel said, 'We have been monitoring this particular investment very closely since it first came to the market. We feel that we have acquired an ultra-prime and prominent piece of Central London freehold at a sensible price. We believe that with some active management this property will fit in very well with the rest of our portfolio.'

Looking back over his successes to date, Sugar said that, despite his having purchased many glamorous and iconic properties, his favourites were often more down-to-earth affairs. 'One of the greatest buildings I ever bought was a warehouse on the intersection of the M25 and A12 fifteen years ago,' he said, with a smile. 'I paid £800,000 for it. My advisers told me I was stupid, and my Jewish advisers called me a *schmuck*. But for ten years it has been paying me more than £500,000 a year in rent.'

Unsurprisingly, he is far from being a fan of agents. 'I pay far too much in agency fees, as I keep telling my son. I have been buying for twenty years and have never sold anything, so one day I will test these people.' He tells a story of an agent who, during a deal to buy property in Park Lane, told him, in an Eton accent, that nobody would pay the prices Sir Alan was hoping for the properties. 'I said to him, in my Hackney accent with a few expletives added, that when the right person comes along and falls in love with the place then they'll pay anything for it. That's exactly what happened.'

No doubt the posh agent scuttled off with his tail firmly between his legs.

'Amsprop is set up more as a family pension fund than a traditional property company,' said Daniel. 'While we are not averse to trading opportunities, our main aim is to hold good-quality freehold property for the long term.'

Nowadays, most of Sir Alan's fortune comes from his property empire. But, there have also been some less successful ventures along the way, such as the Amstrad em@iler. A device that lets you send emails via a fixed-line phone, the em@iler seemed a brilliant idea when it was launched in 1999. At the launch, Sugar revealed that he had made them in China, and jokingly defended this decision, saying, 'My em@ilers are made down the road from Dyson's new factory.' This referred to the vacuum-cleaner tycoon's decision to make his machines in Malaysia.

He employed his son Simon to work on the project. 'Business is business, and family is family, and the two things are kept completely separate with us,' said Simon, who joined at the age of 26. 'He treats me like any other employee, and that's how it should be.'

Launching the product in 1999, Sir Alan said, 'I see the em@iler becoming the "all-in-one communications centre" in the home. It will also be regarded as an "electronic billboard", providing advertisers with a highly cost-effective way of targeting consumers. In true Amstrad tradition, the em@iler brings email to the mass market for the first time in an easy-to-use format at a very affordable price.' Sir Alan said the em@iler would cost £79.99.

However, the initial response was subdued, and more than 17 per cent was wiped off the value of Amstrad shares on the day of the launch. One analyst said, 'The group's new em@iler product may well be a winner, but it would have to be something spectacular to have justified all the hype which has been surrounding this company for several months now.'

Sir Alan dismissed all the negativity, insisting that the 'City scribblers' had got it wrong. 'I am not ready to be put out to grass yet,' he said. 'We have launched enough products over 25 years to know which ones are going to fly off the shelves. You can tell from customers' reaction very early on whether a new product is going to be a winner.' The first batch of 500 em@iler phones were sold out within two days, he said.

However, the press seemed to scent blood in this project and reacted accordingly, slating it on a regular basis. 'Amstrad profit hit by em@iler', claimed the *Daily Mail*. 'Sir Alan Sugar's Amstrad has sold nearly 5,000 em@ilers a week since it went on general sale early this summer. But the heavily subsidised sales, of 70,000 units so far, come at a heavy cost. They knocked £2.3 million off profits in the June year and the costs continue.'

But, in 2002, Sir Alan was still bravely defending the em@iler. 'People say I'm nuts, but the em@iler is as cheap and useful as a phone, before you consider everything else it can do.'

Soon, the picture did indeed appear much brighter.

'Amstrad back in black as em@iler sales improve', announced the *Financial Times* in September 2003 as Amstrad halved the price of the unit.

A spokesman explained the pricing decision: 'The business model is fine but we need more sales.' Commercial director Simon Sugar said, 'The price reduction will be supported by press advertising and in-store promotions and we are confident that this will increase sales significantly. We have had nearly three years' experience of running the em@iler business and the revenue per phone has held up well.'

Things were indeed far rosier than the media suggested: they sold almost 298,000 units and claimed a million users during the first four years of the em@iler's existence. Benefiting from increased subscription revenues and lower production costs, the division turned around from a £5.5 million loss to a £1 million profit on sales of £6.5 million.

However, the media would need a lot of convincing. 'Jury still out on Sir Alan's gadget', said the *Daily Telegraph* in 2004. The jury may be out, but Sir Alan gave his own verdict. 'We launched the first em@iler in the middle of all that Internet bullshit, and when it started to collapse we got dragged down with it. The one thing I learned is that money talks. OK? We are in profit now. That answers all the doubters. We will continue to increase profits. That's the bottom line. You can talk about all that future technology crap, but we are actually in profit and you can't argue with the facts.'

However, by the beginning of 2006, the facts showed that the em@iler was not firing on all cylinders. 'Sugar's em@iler in the firing line as profits fall', said the *Guardian* in February 2006. The same year, Amserve stopped making the product, as reported in the *Evening Standard*: 'Sugar caned as plug pulled on em@iler'.

The media had been harsh on the product, but by this time Sir Alan had become a major media star himself.

CHAPTER EIGHT
THE APPRENTICE

Nowadays, Sugar is such a celebrity and so regularly in the public eye that it may surprise some readers to learn that he was not always so fond of the limelight. Underneath his straight-talking demeanour, Sugar has a distinctly shy side. During the 1980s, as his business reputation increased as a result of his impressive computer sales, he became deluged with offers for television appearances, press interviews and public speaking, often more than 40 requests each month. Most were turned down. Among these were the sorts of offers that many public figures dream of: the producers of iconic BBC radio show *Desert Island Discs*, for instance, came knocking on his door. However, he was somewhat more keen on public speaking and his performances there drew widespread praise.

As we saw in the Preface, his direct and charismatic

way with words when speaking in public made him quite a magnetic orator. Perhaps it was during one of these events that it first dawned on him that one day he could become a television star. The only question was what genre of television would suit a man like him. Fortunately, the broadcast world answered that for him.

The 21st century has seen the genre of reality television become hugely popular, and therefore big business. So it was surely going to be only a matter of time before a reality-television show based on big business would be launched following the phenomenal success of the early reality shows such as *Big Brother*.

In 2000, the first *Big Brother* series to be shown in Britain appeared. As the housemates wheeled their suitcases into the soon-to-be-famous house, television in this country changed for ever. Soon, the music world was muscling in on the reality-television genre, with *Popstars* forming a band in front of television viewers' eyes. With the success of that show, and that of the resultant band Hear'Say, there was soon an even more successful reality music show in the form of *Pop Idol*, followed by Simon Cowell's new talent shows *The X Factor* and *Britain's Got Talent*. Television was 'keeping it real', and the viewers were loving it. But could a reality show based on the world of business be a hit?

But, because of the immediate smash-hit status that *The Apprentice* achieved, it is often forgotten that *Dragons' Den* was, in fact, the first business-based reality-television show in the UK. The format for this show – which originally came from Japan – is wonderfully simple and effective, as contestants pitch business ideas to a panel of multimillionaire entrepreneurs. They ask for investment in their business idea in return for a share of the equity. The contestants set a figure for the investment and equity, though the latter is nearly always the subject of fierce negotiation, should one or more of the Dragons be interested in making an investment. If they are not interested, the Dragons declare this with an often-thunderously delivered declaration: 'I'm out!'

The initial five-person panel for *Dragons' Den* consisted of Simon Woodroffe, Rachel Elnaugh, Doug Richard, Peter Jones and Duncan Bannatyne. The highly charismatic Woodroffe started the Yo! Sushi chain in Britain in 1997, and he has since also become a motivational speaker. Elnaugh founded Red Letter Days, which offered 'experience' gifts, including action events and memorable days out. Richard is a UK-based American involved in technology transfer, commercialisation and business incubation. Jones is a British businessman with interests in mobile telecommunications, television, media, leisure and property. Bannatyne is a Scottish entrepreneur whose many business interests include a successful chain of health clubs.

The show was an immediate success, with the ideas pitched to the Dragons varying from the weird to the wonderful, and the Dragons made for fantastic television. Woodroffe was very much the wild child of the panel, with his snazzy clothes and quirky sideboards. Earlier in his life, he had been on the road with rock acts including Rod Stewart and it showed in his cool manner. Richard was the most outspoken of the original panel, and his bluntness sometimes bordered on the rude, which gave proceedings a real edge. Peter Jones was tall, posh and telegenic. He has since become a very tough talker himself, but back in the early days he was more fair and measured in his response. Bannatyne was amusing, entertaining and wise from the off, and, along with Jones, has since become a fixture of the ever-changing panel. Amid all this testosterone, Elnaugh sometimes seemed a bit out of place and her very involvement was soon to become one of the series' first controversies and made some wonder whether she really could be considered a true Dragon.

Meanwhile, the ideas were often entertaining in their own right. For the viewer, all this was absolutely gripping television. We cheered on those who we felt deserved investment, and sneered at those whose ideas or pitches – or both! – were terrible. But even those who made the programme admit they have been surprised by how successful the show has become. As presenter Evan Davis said, 'Few could have predicted just how many interesting characters there are in the business world, or how much drama a televised investment encounter can generate.'

The critics agreed wholeheartedly. Ben Marshall in the *Guardian Guide* wrote, '[The show] is a brilliant bit of scheduling. Vast numbers of businesses, mostly unsuccessful, are conceived by people lying among carnival debris with a monstrous hangover. In *Dragons' Den*, young men and women pitch their ideas to a group of savagely sceptical multimillionaires. It makes for horribly compelling viewing and is particularly painful for anyone who has ever spent time trying to convince a roomful of obscenely rich men to part with their cash.'

The hard-nosed Victor Lewis-Smith, writing in the *Evening Standard*, said, 'Combining hard-headed commerce and innovative design with *Pop Idol*-style humiliation, it's provided compelling viewing . . . as five fairly knowledgeable and highly opinionated multimillionaires have poured scorn and ridicule on inventions that either don't work or aren't needed, before occasionally agreeing to put their money where their mouth is.'

The *Western Daily Press* commented, '*Dragons' Den* is a sort of *Pop Idol* for would-be entrepreneurs, except all the judges are Mr Nasty types. Hard-eyed and unsmiling, they put the poor supplicants through the kind of humiliation you used to get when you dared ask the bank manager for a loan to extend the conservatory.' The review concluded, 'Move over, Simon Cowell. You have competition.'

The first series was, indeed, peculiarly entertaining. In

subsequent years, those who pitched ideas had had the chance to watch the show, and therefore knew full well what they were letting themselves in for. But, in the first series, the pitchers were very much lambs to the slaughter. As presenter Davis put it, 'I had always felt rather sorry for those entrepreneurs who came into the Den in the first series – they had never been able to watch the programme and see what they were in for.'

The same can be said of the line-up for the first series of the next business reality show to be launched: *The Apprentice*. As with all reality shows, in subsequent series those who took part were more savvy as to how the show worked, but those who put themselves up for the first year had only a very vague idea of what was in store for them. Therefore, for them – and the viewer – it was a particularly intriguing and fresh experience. Nobody outside the production team knew exactly what hurdles and tasks were ahead, nor how the whole tone and energy of the process would manifest itself.

However, *The Apprentice* was an entirely new phenomena, as there had already been a successful series of *The Apprentice* in America, broadcast on the NBC channel in the winter of 2004. Billed as 'The Ultimate Job Interview' in the 'Ultimate Jungle', the show pitched businesspeople against one another in an elimination-style competition for a one-year $250,000 starting contract, running one of the companies owned by US billionaire Donald Trump. Trump has made much of his fortune through property development and casino ownership and his name is synonymous with the rough and tumble of business success. He's a very charismatic and ebullient figure – perfect for a show such as *The Apprentice*. 'I'm not a big fan of the handshake,' he told US TV channel NBC. 'I think it's barbaric, shaking hands, you catch colds, you catch the flu, you catch this, you catch all sorts of things.' With the outspoken and flamboyant way he had about him, the man they call The Donald makes for magnetic television, as viewers of the original *Apprentice* series soon discovered. The US series began with sixteen contestants, eight men and eight women from around America, all of whom had been successful in various professional enterprises, including real estate, restaurant management, political consulting and sales. During the show, the contestants lived communally in a suite on the fourth floor of Trump Tower in Manhattan. In the now familiar format, elimination consisted of one contestant being 'fired' by Trump at the conclusion of each week's episode. Filming of the entire series took just three months. The result was a huge success, with the show averaging at number seven in the weekly viewing charts, and average viewing figures of 20.7 million viewers each week. This was a godsend for NBC, because the channel's two big hitters – comedies *Frasier* and *Friends* – were coming to an end.

Soon, broadcasters in the United Kingdom who had watched the show and its success saw the potential for a

UK version. The BBC were first to reveal an interest. 'We are still in advanced negotiations about *The Apprentice*. But there have been some ideas discussed, one of which is that [then BBC director general] Greg Dyke might be very good as part of the panel [of judges],' a spokeswoman said. 'But we would not consider Greg for the Donald Trump character, and not if he went to ITV.'

Soon, a bidding war erupted over which network would get the rights to *The Apprentice*. BBC2 and Channel 4 both bid fiercely for the rights to the show, but BBC2 came out on top. Although Philip Green was reportedly considered for the top job, the choice of Alan Sugar was undoubtedly the correct one. He had a back catalogue of experience of television thanks to the many interviews and other appearances he had had to make while working at Tottenham Hotspur. Also, as one executive involved said, if Richard Branson had been chosen, he wouldn't have been able to stop smiling, even as he was firing someone.

So it was that Sir Alan got the nod. '*The Apprentice* is a 12-week crash course in business survival techniques. Grounded in commercial reality, it is not for the faint-hearted,' he said. 'It doesn't claim to turn everyone into an entrepreneur.'

Why had the man with a shy side, who was often known to ooze with contempt for the media, chosen to sign up? 'I'd been involved with the government in visiting schools and promoting enterprise among young people, and this opportunity slotted nicely into that,' he said. 'Plus, I knew the US *Apprentice* had taken off, and had a tremendous impact on business awareness. I'm sure they knocked on all the usual suspects' doors before they got to me, but, while some businessmen may be clever and bright, they can dry up in front of a camera. I'd been on so many *Money Programme*s and faced the cameras constantly when I was chairman of Tottenham Hotspur, and I made it clear that I thought *The Apprentice* was something I could do.'

It wasn't something he did for the money on a personal level, because he donates his appearance fee to charity. 'I really think it opens a window into the business world, and that's why I do it,' he said forcefully. 'I know that top businessmen profess to think it's all a bit of a joke, but, while they're sitting there calling the candidates a bunch of pricks, they're all glued to the programme. But I also know for an undisputed fact that kids from 11 to 15 are the biggest audience. They love it and learn from it.'

The opening series was broadcast on 16 February 2005, when we were introduced to the first batch of contestants, who were initially divided into teams of men, named Impact, and women, First Forte, and it was clear from the off that there were plenty of entertaining characters involved.

Adele, 29, was the manager of a lucrative property development company. She was also the general manager of a family firm, something that Sugar could relate to because he has employed relatives at Amstrad since the earliest days. She famously worked into the evening the night before she gave birth, and sold a kitchen to her midwife during labour. It was clear from the off that here was a straight-talking candidate.

Adenike was a year older than Adele and was just as self-assured. Owning and managing a restaurant and running huge events for top-notch corporate clients, she was clearly a smart character. Her determination and intense focus promised to ensure she was one to watch in situations of potential conflict.

An internal communications manger for an oil company, 35-year-old Lindsay was not as quick to shout about her ambition as other candidates, but she insisted that didn't mean she lacked that quality.

Glamorous Miranda was a 26-year-old managing director of a commission-based estate agency. Having already launched two successful companies, she claimed to have been a saleswoman since the tender age of 12. A previous manager said of Miranda that 'her sales technique and the profits she generated for the company remain legendary'. The question mark was whether, behind her brilliant presentational skills, there was any substance in this candidate. Time would tell. Miriam had made a 20-hour round trip to attend each stage of the interview process to get through to appear on *The Apprentice*, underlining her motivation: 'It's an investment for the future,' she explained.

Rachel, a fundraising manager for one of the largest national children's charities, was bubbly and charismatic.

Then there was Saira. A corporate sales manager for an online recruitment company, she was full of drive and energy. So strong was her self-belief and confidence that she delayed her wedding plans in order to take part in *The Apprentice*. 'I hope that as an Asian woman I will give other Asian women the inspiration to go out there and do well in business,' she declared. A gym freak, she also spoke four languages as well as English – Bhari, Urdu, Punjabi and Hindu. This was fitting, for she was without doubt the most talkative of the candidates. Would she be too chatty for her own good? Would she play as good a game as she talked?

First up for the guys was the smooth and sophisticated Ben. A handsome, charismatic man, he ran his own headhunting firm, a field he had worked in since the age of 17. His pedigree was undeniable, and he had once been voted Global Consultant of the Year.

Another suave operator was James, a former public-school boy who lived by the maxim 'I seek success as a result of my own achievements'. He was no stranger to business-related competitions, having previously been a finalist in *Property Week*'s Young Property Personality of the Year. Articulate and posh, from the start James seemed destined to be a particularly memorable candidate, and so it was to prove.

Sebastian, another posh boy, was a Savile Row-suited corporate finance man.

The oldest candidate was 39-year-old former

Conservative parliamentary candidate Matthew, who was more than a little eccentric. Tall and brimming with enthusiasm, he admitted from the off that diplomacy was not his strong point, which proved to be something of an understatement. That said, Sir Alan himself said that he knew how it felt to be accused of having an attitude problem, so he was not about to automatically write Matthew off.

Raj was the founder and managing director of an estate agency. He had a business failure on his record, but Sir Alan said he would not hold this against a candidate in whom he recognised plentiful entrepreneurial characteristics.

'I know I'm not the cleverest bloke in business, so I always make sure I check everything, and then I check and check again,' said 34-year-old Paul, introducing himself to the viewing public. But he was being a little hard on himself, for, as would become very quickly apparent, Paul was a born salesman. Sir Alan said he recognised a lot of his younger self in Paul. With a potential to erupt into temper, Paul was one to watch.

The opening words of Tim Campbell were not without confidence. 'Sir Alan has a lot he could teach me. Perhaps I might know a few things that I could teach him as well.' With a sharp eye and a charismatic presence, Tim was also a man who managed to become popular quickly, making him a fine team player. Even without the benefit of hindsight, it was clear that this young man was going to be a major contender.

The first task appeared simple enough: the two teams were sent out to buy and sell flowers, and the team who made the more money would be crowned winners, and, in the now famous words to the losing team, 'one of you will get fired'.

Saira headed the First Forte team, and Tim headed the Impact team. First Forte began by selling flowers at a market before deciding to sell on the street. Impact, on the other hand, immediately started selling flowers door to door and won the task. While they celebrated on the London Eye, Saira's First Forte team were dragged into the dreaded boardroom. Sir Alan chewed over the options of whom to dismiss, before finally deciding. He pointed his finger at Adenike and uttered the immortal *Apprentice* line, 'You're fired!'

Week two's task was to design a new product for a toy company. Impact won again, not least because the First Forte team leader Lindsay did not listen to her colleagues and instead went with a bizarre product called 'Secret Signals'.

Sugar decided to mix up the teams, and, after two further victories by the Impact team (one on a purchasing task, the other on a selling task), the show had lost two more women: Adele and Miranda. Then, First Forte finally won its first task in an entertaining episode. The teams had been asked to choose an artist and sell their work at an art gallery. First Forte brought back £19,563 to the boardroom. Although Impact had sold more paintings, their artist's work sold less per work and as a result they netted just £6,147. So it was that the first man of the series – Matthew – heard the words, 'You're fired!'

First Forte were the winners the following week, too, when their task had been to design an advertisement for the Amstrad jukebox music system and pitch it to firms. In what proved to be a hilarious episode, advertising woman Rachel performed a bizarre pitch that involved her throwing her shoes across the room and dancing in a manner that could at best be described as eccentric. Paul, Saira and – inevitably – Rachel were taken into the boardroom. Rachel was the contestant to be fired but Sugar also scolded Paul and Saira, who had been arguing constantly.

If Rachel had shown herself up herself in that episode, then many of the contestants matched her performance in the following week. The task here was to negotiate with five celebrities and persuade them to donate their property or services for a charity auction in aid of the refurbishment of Hackney Empire, back in Sir Alan's old stomping ground. One of the celebrities was Paul McKenna, and Raj chose to lead the negotiations, as he was a confirmed fan of the celebrity hypnotist. In the event, Raj was utterly starstruck and rambled embarrassingly at McKenna until Paul intervened and took over the pitch. Meanwhile, Tim managed to offend

Ian Wright during their negotiations and he had to be bailed out by Miriam. On the night of the auction, there was more toe-curling when the theatre tickets donated by comedian Mel Smith almost failed to sell. Ben's Impact team won the night, by raising £18,000 to First Forte's £10,000. James, Raj and Sebastian went into the boardroom, and Sebastian was the next to be shown the door.

Ben was fired in week eight after a task that involved selling food at a country market. The winning team – First Forte – were given as their reward a trip to Monaco, where they were allowed to gamble their task profits at a swish casino.

Week nine saw Saira at her entertaining and enraging best. The task was to market a text-messaging service to fans of Sugar's old club, Tottenham Hotspur. Saira was far too pushy towards the club marketing manager and relations between both teams and the club suffered hugely as a result. Paul's Impact team beat Saira's First Forte team, and Saira came within a whisker of being fired in the boardroom, but in the end it was Raj who was dismissed, because he had once more failed to take throw himself sufficiently into the task.

Miriam was sacked at the end of the next task, which involved selling products on a shopping channel, despite her highly accomplished presenting performance. But she had failed to keep control of her team, with Paul proving to be particularly livewire.

And so to the semifinals, where each of the remaining candidates – James, Paul, Saira and Tim – were grilled by a panel of tough interviewers hired by Sir Alan. James and Paul failed to impress the interviewers and were both fired. Paul was considered too aggressive, and there were question marks as to whether he truly wished to be the Apprentice, which was also the main reason for James's dismissal. So, the show had its final two: the dependable Tim and the entertaining Saira.

It was to prove to be an engaging final, with fired candidates brought back to the show to help, as Tim and Saira went head to head each organising an event on a riverboat. Saira put on a wine-tasting night, while Tim held a fashion show. Naturally, Sir Alan turned up to both evenings. Here, the winner was not determined merely by who did better financially from the task (in which case, Saira would have been hired). Instead, the overall performance and long-term visions of the candidates were taken into account. In the boardroom, having considered all the aspects, Sir Alan pointed at Tim and said, 'You're hired!' *The Apprentice* had crowned its first winner.

Sugar admitted that he had looked forward to the moment in the series when, instead of saying the negative 'You're fired!', he could instead utter 'You're hired.' He had known from the off that there would be occasions where it would be 'heartbreaking' to have to tell a contestant they were fired. 'You'd be an iron-cold person if you said it doesn't matter,' he admitted. Indeed, he has revealed, one of the few non-negotiable aspects of his part on the show is that he has to utter the line exactly the same way every week. 'Personally, I'd have liked the flexibility to be able to vary it, to say, "You're sacked!" or "Get out!" or possibly even "Clear off!"' He shrugs. 'But they tell me "You're fired!" is great TV.' However, lest we conclude he was turning soft, he added, 'On the other hand, there are certain types of people I have no trouble firing: the lazy, the incompetent, the disloyal.' He also enjoyed telling Tim that he was the winner, and therefore hired.

However, all involved in the series were winners, as it proved to be extremely successful. The viewer ratings were impressive, at first averaging around 2.5 million, with this figure climbing to around 4 million viewers by the end of the series. The critical reception was also pleasing for all involved. The *Sun* said dubbed it 'the thinking man's reality show', and the *Mirror* described it as 'jaw-dropping viewing'. Broadsheet newspapers seemed head-over-heels for the programme, too, with the *Daily Telegraph* calling it 'the most addictive show in years', and the *Guardian* saying that it provided 'a salutary lesson in aggressive buying and selling, hiring and firing'. The *Sunday Times* said that it was 'not just a game show: it's a business school'. The *Evening Standard* also praised it, describing the programme as 'terribly compelling'.

Journalist James Brown was also suitably impressed. Writing in the *Independent*, he gushed, 'There is a feeling among reality-TV experts that *The Apprentice* may be the best programme of its genre ever shown on British television. It has all the trappings of core reality programming: a group of ordinary people who want something and are tested on television to get it.' Given the glut of reality-television shows, this was high praise indeed.

Brown then turned his pen to the star of the show: 'Then it has its honey-trap character, a magnetic personality who emerges during the series and stealthily gets you obsessed. This person, naturally, is Sugar: a rough-and-ready, straight-talking, self-made East End trader, manufacturer and landlord who has honed his instinct for a deal into a billion-dollar business. On top of this the programme-makers have shot London from the air in the style of Hollywood legends Michael Mann and David Fincher, and added a soundtrack that ratchets up the tension.'

The first series won a host of awards including the Most Popular Reality Show at the 2005 National Television Awards. Sugar has since said that he had foreseen all this popularity. He explained that, on starting work on it, he quickly realised just how exciting and successful the show was going to be. Asked if he expected it to become a hit, he said, 'Yes, I did actually. Not when they first asked me, but when I could see how it was going from the slices I was shown by the production crew. What you see is me, there's no acting, and the same goes for the apprentices. It has been an amazing experience, in that I've learned about the world of television and how to make a TV programme. Hats off to the production team, because for every one of those episodes, there must have been 35 hours of film. They've had to watch it all and edit it down. The BBC have spent money on quality; then again, they'll be able to use those opening shots again in a second series. Would I do a second series? Yes.'

However, on the question of scheduling, he was somewhat more critical of the Beeb. 'If I have any criticism of the BBC, it is only that they picked a poor night by scheduling it on Wednesday, because it clashes with the Champions League. The first few weeks they were ecstatic, because they were attracting the elusive audience of 29- to 35-year-old boyos, the yuppies, the upwardly mobile aspiring boyos. But then these guys also have Sky Plus, so I think we're losing a lot of the audience figures to people who are watching it an hour later, after the football.' He then moved closer to home to underline his point. 'I can give you no better example than my own two sons. Last week they watched Chelsea–Arsenal first on Sky, and then their dad afterwards on Sky Plus.' He added with a grin, 'That's loyalty for you.'

He was also critical when he discovered that journalists who were interviewing him ahead of the screening of the final had not been allowed to know who won as they did those interviews. 'Wha-aa-at?' he stormed on discovering this. 'Bloody comedians, they are! What is the point of your seeing the bloody thing? I mean, the whole action's at the end. You're supposed to come here with an understanding of the programme and they've only given you a quarter of the story.' He asked after the PR who had made this decision: 'Who is this fool? I'll get him on the phone!'

However, overall he was very much enjoying the show and happy with how it turned out. 'It's 80 per cent business and 20 per cent fun,' he told one interviewer. 'If you saw the American one – which I thought was crap – and then you see with ours that there's less glitz and showbiz here. You can follow what's going on. The American one – the business side – was very hard to follow.'

What had been easy to follow was the form of the eventual winner, Tim Campbell, who had been mild-mannered and professional throughout. When others became melodramatic, insulting or wild, Campbell kept his head down and got on with the job in hand. Some therefore argued that he did not deserve to win, because they felt he kept his head far *too* down, to the extent that he was trying to keep himself out of the firing line. Campbell faced these allegations head on. He told the press, 'The criticism thrown at me is that I kind of disappear. But a big part of business is to observe. There's no point shouting very loudly when there are 13 other people shouting very loudly themselves.'

Fiery candidate Paul Torrisi put the boot in, too, when he suggested that the final pairing were selected to satisfy a politically correct manifesto. 'It still hurts I didn't get to the last two,' he said, frowning. 'Saira and Tim – Asian girl against black kid from east London – it just smacked of the BBC a bit; it annoys me. There were people I bloody hated. Saira was the obvious one I didn't get on with; it got to the stage where we were bickering at every opportunity.'

But Tim's story was in fact inspirational stuff. He revealed that his motivation came from very close to home, in a drive to make his mother proud of him. 'There are lots of statistics about single-parent families, and my mother, Una, was determined we wouldn't be statistics,' he declared. 'I'm the eldest of three and my mum took on three jobs to make sure we had everything we needed. One of my driving forces is to make her proud. To see her face when I appeared on TV was priceless. I can never repay her for what she did, but just to be able to give her some peace of mind and show people that she was a good mother has made me one of the happiest people in the world.'

Of course, he was also happy to have won, and took the opportunity to look back over the filming of the series and give an insight into what went on behind the scenes during his *Apprentice* experience. 'When I sent off the application, I didn't think that much of it,' he said, shrugging. 'I didn't realise the beast I was unleashing in terms of being part of the *Apprentice* machine. I remember being picked up from my east London home in a black Mercedes and being dropped off outside the boardroom. Then we were introduced to Sir Alan with his famous opening line, "I don't like liars, I don't like bullshitters." It will always stick in my head.

'There were no snobs in the house,' adds the man that became Sir Alan's first Apprentice. 'I think the producers anticipated it being like the American show, with lots of bitchiness, but it really wasn't like that.' That said, there was plenty of direct talk among the candidates, as is surely befitting a show with straight-talking Sir Alan at the helm. Campbell agreed. 'I come from a world where everything is politically correct. Being in a situation where things are actually expressed was quite refreshing. It may seem brutal, but for me it was always fair.'

He was asked whether he believed that Sugar ever make a wrong decision. 'When he got rid of Ben,' Tim replied. 'Yes, Ben made a mistake in not setting a budget [in the farmers' market task], but I think there was more of him to be seen. As a potential employee, Ben wasn't a bad choice.'

And, given that she made the final, the same could presumably be said of Saira, and no one could have criticised her work rate, which was tireless. Her personality, however, had regularly bubbled over and become too intense and in your face. So, looking back, was she shocked when she witnessed on the small screen how she had behaved? 'When I first saw it, I did think, "Oh, my word!"' Saira admitted. 'I was a bit taken aback. But I've learned a lot from seeing myself. I understand now what people mean when they say, "Your energy really annoys me" – because I don't shut up.'

Turning to where she got her own drive from, it was a less happy story than Campbell's. 'My father was a very strong figure,' Saira recalled. 'He never, ever praised us. If I got a B at school, he would ask why I didn't get an A. I was never good enough, and that's what drove me. I wanted to prove something to him, I suppose.'

Although she had not won the series, she had proved a strong point by running the winner so close.

The two finalists are still in touch to this day. 'I still keep up with Saira [Khan],' Tim said in 2008. 'She's doing brilliant stuff and I love her to death. We share this thing – it was almost like being kidnapped together. I still get approached a fair bit, it's part and parcel of it. But I still shop at my local supermarket and I don't have a butler.'

Some argued that it was society at large that was the true winner. Leo McKinstry wrote a moving and rousing tribute to the show in the *Daily Mail*. 'Indeed, *The Apprentice* runs against the fashionable values, not just of the BBC, but of our entire society. In our culture of grievance, with its shrill emphasis on employee rights, it is wonderfully refreshing to have a programme that does not treat its participants as victims and does not regard pressure as a dirty word. In a world of compensation and industrial tribunals, where it is virtually impossible to sack any public employee, no matter how incompetent, it is a pleasant shock to hear failure met with the phrase: "You're fired!" Those words contain a beautiful, unemotional purity. At least in *The Apprentice*, if not in Labour's Britain – or more specifically, in Tony Blair's government – individuals are held to account for their performances.'

Producer Michele Kurland said, 'I think the reason *The Apprentice* is so popular is that, unlike shows like *Big Brother*, it's not designed to be egg-on-face TV. It's about humanising business so that viewers can empathise with the candidates' plight when things go wrong, as they invariably do. You really start to root for these people as the series progresses.

'A lot of thought has gone into the programme's look and feel. The feeling was, if you're talking about business to a UK audience, who sometimes perceive it as grey, then you should glam it up, make it big and glossy. It's aspirational, so it should look amazing. We have a huge team working on the show, and to me it's like a massive orchestra giving this amazing performance.'

They certainly did, not least by Alan Sugar in the boardroom scenes of *The Apprentice*. Thankfully, there was to be plenty more where that came from.

Sugar's television appearances are almost invariably entertaining, but they are always met with varying responses from TV critics. In 2005, he appeared on BBC's comedy show *Room 101*, where guests are allowed to consign things they dislike to that infamous room. Among the items Sugar chose were men who wear wigs, and, when host Paul Merton showed Sugar a photograph of Donald Trump, who, as we know, fronted the American version of the series, his guest rolled out a smooth anecdote. He explained how, while filming an episode of *The Apprentice*, he had been filmed on a speedboat. 'I said to [the crew], "Trump couldn't do this," and they said, "Why not?" and I said, " 'Cos his bloody hair would be back there at Tower Bridge."'

Graham Young, TV editor of the *Birmingham Mail*, wrote, 'Sir Alan Sugar makes an interesting choice for *Room 101*. Never short of an opinion or two, he tells Merton that his pet hates include professional schmoozers and men with wigs.' The Scottish *Daily Record* made Sir Alan's edition their pick of the day, as did London's *Evening Standard*, saying, 'Host Paul Merton spars wittily with the grumpy businessman.' The *Glasgow Evening Times* also made it their choice of the day, saying, 'The prospect of Sir Alan sitting across from Paul Merton on a show about pet hates is a tantalising prospect indeed.' The *Sun* picked it out as 'What to watch tonight', although their description of it was not entirely flattering: 'Sir Alan Sugar shot to TV fame as the

Nookie Bear/Sid James lookalike in top reality show *The Apprentice*, uttering those immortal words: You're fired! He always did look grumpy and, tonight, as he joins Paul Merton to discuss his pet hates, he proves he really is.'

But *The Times* was definitely not complimentary. David Chater roared, 'Prickly, glum and egotistical, Sir Alan Sugar is like Sid James without the laughs, and he makes Paul Merton struggle to generate any lightness or humour.' Thomas Sutcliffe, writing in the *Independent* also put the boot in: 'I know they'd never allow *Room 101* itself to be consigned to the chute but occasionally you get a guest who makes things a bit uncomfortable for a while, and Sir Alan Sugar was one of them. You get the feeling that people don't interrupt Sir Alan's anecdotes often, so he has, to put it tactfully, evolved a notion of comic rhythm different than most people's. Listening to him dawdle through an underpowered story, the punchline of which was designed to show Sir Alan in a flattering light, Merton twitched with frustration, like a man in a Ferrari blocked in behind a steam-roller.'

The critics may not have all enjoyed the performance, but, as ever, Sugar had reached out to the people who mattered – the ordinary viewers. In the *Edinburgh Evening News*'s 'Have your say' section, Sarah Howell of Trinity, said, 'I liked seeing the *Room 101* with Sir Alan Sugar again. He's a very sharp guy with a wicked sense of humour and I was in stitches by the end. I hope they bring back the show soon because it's one of the best programmes over the past few years.' (Indeed, Sugar is both a popular and terrifying television figure, if a 2006 *Radio Times* poll is to be believed, where he was voted the seventh scariest celebrity on television, beaten by Gordon Ramsay and Anne Robinson.)

Ever since the end of the first series of *The Apprentice*, fans had been eagerly awaiting the second instalment, and, in February 2006, their wait was finally over, as the second series hit our screens. The candidates' accommodation was a 7,000-square-foot converted glass factory in Battersea. There was also a new boardroom, described as 'aqueous' in the *Daily Telegraph*. In time, Sugar would be a little bit more dynamic and abrasive in Series 2. But the strengths of the show established in Series 1 were all still very much in evidence. It was immediately clear that, once again, the house was to be chock-full of characters. Two contestants who quickly stood out as such were 31-year-old Syed Ahmed (as one online blogger put it, 'Syed could start a fight in an empty house') and the lively Jo Cameron, who had set her own business up in 2004 after being made redundant and, from the off, looked set to be the second series' eccentric.

By now, behind-the-scenes details of the show were forthcoming, and being lapped up by *Apprentice* addicts. For instance, it was revealed that the fired candidates' 'walk of shame' from the office to taxi was not actually filmed after they have been fired. Instead, all 14 contestants were filmed walking into the cab on the first day of filming, then footage of each 'walk' was added into individual episodes. More significantly, despite the show suggesting that the hiring and firing was done in an office in Canary Wharf, Sir Alan's office was in reality based in the somewhat less glamorous surroundings of Brentwood in Essex.

Not that any of this detracted from the sheer enjoyment of the show. This series quickly produced one of the most memorable episodes to date. In Episode 2, the two teams competed to raise money for Sugar's chosen cause, the Great Ormond Street Hospital. Each team were ordered to design a calendar, price it and then sell it wholesale to real buyers from three of Britain's leading retailers. It turned into a hilarious episode, particularly when it came to the appalling pitches the teams made to the buyers. Nargis was chosen to make the presentation for the girls' team, and it is hard to imagine how she could have made a worse, or more hilariously bad, job of it.

Sugar himself was stunned by her performance. 'I couldn't believe the arrogant way she alienated the buyers,' he said. 'She clearly had no idea that buyers for the big chains and stores should be shown some respect. They get hundreds of people trying to sell them stuff every day. You have to convince them they need to buy your product, that it will fly off the shelves.'

Sugar felt Mani's pitch was better, but not ideal, as he had focused too much on the charity aspect. A memorable moment came when one of the buyers gave Mani the figure of how many calendars they sold each year, and Mani interrupted, as flatteringly as it is possible to imagine, saying, 'Sorry, just a moment: *wow*!' It was one of those cringe-making but totally unmissable television moments.

The boys' team won and were given a caviar tasting as a treat, while Nargis was justly fired for her terrible presentation.

Another memorable moment came the following week, when Sugar told Jo that he was not sure that she wasn't 'just a bloody nutter'. Jo took this in her stride. 'I am loud, annoying and emotional,' she admitted, during the boardroom showdown, when she came within an inch of being fired herself that week, but impressed Sir Alan with her vigorous self-defence.

Week 4 saw a major cock-up from Syed in a food-stall task. They were making 90 chicken tikka pizzas, and Syed vastly overordered, bringing in a total of 300 chickens. Sugar's dryly witty adviser Nick Hewer asked Syed whether he felt he had perhaps ordered a few too many. The task produced a spectacular boardroom showdown, in which Sugar said that, if the rules had allowed him, he would have sacked not just Syed, but all three of the bottom three candidates. Syed put up a spectacular defence and managed to survive to fight another week, despite Sugar holding him '100 per cent responsible' for his team's failure in the task.

'Thank you, Sir Alan,' said Syed as he left the boardroom, a saved man. 'Thank you for the opportunity.'

Sugar snapped, 'Cheeky sod.'

A fellow contestant of Syed was quick to defend him. 'It's high-pressured,' said contestant Tuan Lé. 'You make all those decisions which people think are stupid – like Syed ordering 300 chickens – because you're knackered.'

Indeed, some observers wondered whether Sugar secretly respected Syed's cheek, and saw something of himself in the candidate. Certainly, Syed had a very noble streak in him, although the main evidence of this never made the final cut. In week eight, Syed was responsible for his team arriving late to the boardroom, but Sir Alan, so impressed by Syed's selling prowess, offered him immunity. Syed turned down the chance for immunity, and bravely put himself forward for firing alongside his team-mates. For the final cut, the entire segment was edited out. The series editor, Dan Adamson, said there was no conspiracy behind this editing. 'We weren't deliberately making Syed look bad. The scene just didn't fit,' he said.

In Week 10, Syed was finally shown the door after his failure in the cruise-liner task.

After the traditional interviews round in Week 11, the grand finale saw an all-female affair with Michelle Dewberry coming head to head with Ruth Badger. The pair had to put on an event of their choice at London's Tower Bridge. The series ended with Michelle crowned winner, even though Ruth Badger's sales ability had been phenomenal throughout the series. However, 'the Badger' – who went on to find fame and success off the back of her *Apprentice* run – was gracious in defeat. Dewberry, said Badger, made for a more likely apprentice. 'She's mouldable, whereas I've given up a golden career for the chance. For both of us it's about learning.'

Again, there were suggestions that Sugar had chosen the more bland candidate as his winner, but Dewberry said, 'They underplayed me on screen all the way through so it would be a real shock when I made it into a final. I'm not as dull and quiet as I've been edited to seem.'

Dan Adamson, *The Apprentice*'s editor, maintains that the editing is fair and that 'Sir Alan especially' would never let *The Apprentice* become a sexed-up reality show. However, one ousted contestant, Sharon McAllister, said, 'It's bullshit to describe it as a business programme. It's entertainment. Everything is edited according to Sir Alan's final decision. I was made out to be a whinger and I'm not.'

Badger was more amusing about her surprise on watching the edited programmes. 'Watching it afterwards, there were loads of things I cringed about. Why I look like a bulldog chewing a wasp for the first three weeks I have no idea. And the stupid outfits they made you wear – my life!'

On screen, when a person is 'fired', they go through one door, their team-mates through another, supposedly separated for ever. In fact, the door the fired competitor goes through leads nowhere in particular and all the contestants meet again in an anteroom where, according to McAllister, 'they have a coffee and a natter' before the fired candidate leaves.

As for Dewberry, the girl from Hull has had mixed fortunes since winning the show. Naturally, she became something of a celebrity and so the press were full of stories when it transpired that she was pregnant by fellow contestant Syed Ahmed (she later lost the baby). As more and more reports of her private life hit the press, it was claimed that Sugar was angered by this trend. 'Sir Alan made it clear he's not happy,' a friend of Dewberry's reportedly told the *Sun*. 'It wasn't working out, even before she got pregnant. 'They agreed Michelle will take time off while they sort things out. Her future is in the balance. Sir Alan's on his yacht and they'll talk when he returns.'

Dewberry has since left Amstrad, written an autobiography and formed her own company. She has had cordial conversations with Sugar since and there appear to be no hard feelings. In 2008, she told reporters, 'I've been chatting to Sir Alan and getting his advice about my new online project. He's told me to do my homework and make sure I'm properly prepared before I launch. I'm securing funding at the moment. I speak to him a fair bit and called up to see how he was after his plane crash' (see Chapter 9).

Series 3 of *The Apprentice* kicked off in March 2007 with a now familiar feel to it. The opening titles played out to the theme tune of Prokofiev's 'Dance of the Knight', as the candidates were introduced one by one to the viewing public. Dru Masters, the musical director of the series, explains how they came by this choice. 'We decided early on that, musically, the programme would have a slightly sixties-seventies caper-movie feel, sort of *The Italian Job* meets *Ocean's Eleven*,' he said. 'We had no music for the opening titles. They were thinking of running some kind of M People-style "inspirational" pop song, which I thought would have been disastrous. So I played them the Prokofiev march out of desperation. And suddenly it was like it had always been there. It provides this suitably bombastic backdrop for Sir Alan to ham it up.'

It proved to have the most colourful and controversial line-up of candidates of any series to date, and top of this list from the start was feisty Katie Hopkins. She was to bring huge controversy to the series, with her bitchy remarks behind the backs of her fellow candidates, and her dramatic exit from the competition. Described as a 'power-dressing villainess' by the *Daily Mail*, she earned £90,000 as a brand consultant, and seemed determined to become a brand herself on the show. Among her memorable criticisms of her fellow contestants, she claimed that Adam Hosker's best friends were 'Mr Pinot and Mr Grigio', and blasted Kristina Grimes's 'orange fake tan'. She also expressed a wish that a fellow candidate would 'run over' or go back 'to the North and his Northern chums, where I do feel he rather belongs'. All the while, she made headline-grabbing statements, including boasting that she was 'ten out of ten' in bed, and she was photographed in the newspapers, naked and making love in a cornfield with colleague Mark Cross.

Despite this controversy, she did very well in the tasks and was all set for a place in the final. However, at the end of the penultimate episode, she stepped down from the competition, citing childcare concerns. Watched by 6.2 million viewers, this became an iconic *Apprentice* episode. Soon after awarding her a place in the final, Sugar seemed perturbed and told her, 'You don't look like a lady who's just been told you've entered the final. Everyone would appreciate it if you spoke up.'

Hopkins then shocked him by saying, 'I'm making a decision without having the courtesy to speak to the people who care for my children. It's a risk, it's a discourtesy to my parents.'

Sir Alan angrily hit back, saying, 'I haven't got time to wait for you to make a phone call.'

Following a pause, Hopkins said, 'I don't want to make a fool of you or me. I think it's more important to get the courtesy to have my plans in place, so I'll have to stand down.'

There were suggestions in some quarters that Hopkins had stood down after being pressurised by Sugar about her childcare plans. An *Apprentice* spokesman swatted these claims away. 'As part of the interview process, Sir Alan and his colleagues interrogated all of the candidates about their commitment to the process and the job. He wanted to put them under pressure to be able to be fully confident that they were serious about the opportunity he was offering them. Sir Alan was intent on ensuring that he did not take on an Apprentice who later pulled out due to lack of commitment. Some of the candidates – including Simon Ambrose – were therefore asked about their living and family arrangements.'

Another theory was that Hopkins had never intended to win the show, but merely wanted to use it to gain fame for herself. She was, several fellow contestants claimed, aiming to become a Simon Cowell-esque figure, not Sir Alan's Apprentice. As for Sugar himself, he had described Hopkins as 'an alpha female'. Looking back at her performance, he shook his head and said, 'She's a clever woman, but she went for the short-term cash-in.'

Nick Hewer was similarly dismissive. 'Silly girl,' he said, shrugging. 'She was kind of five degrees off normal, wasn't she? Extraordinary.'

Despite awarding Hopkins a place in the final, Sugar is insistent that she was not, contrary to the assumptions of some observers, about to win the competition. 'She was never ever, ever going to win,' he insisted forcefully. 'Never in a million years. It sounds contradictory and it takes someone with big balls to see through it, but she was there for all the wrong reasons.' Therefore, he says, he deliberately put her on the spot to see how she would react. 'My answer was to lay it on thick. There was a lot of pressure on her in order to flush her out. I knew if I piled it on, she would throw in the towel. Then she started to back out, she realised she was not dealing with a mug. I suppose one does regret having her on the show. She did provide great entertainment to the public, but she was a disappointment.'

Hopkins became a hated public figure, who was booed wildly when she appeared on the aftermath show *You're Fired* on BBC2. She shrugged off the boos, saying, 'The pantomime villain lives on!' Speaking later, she said that she had no regrets at all about her behaviour. 'I'd do it all again, and that includes the aftermath,' she said, smiling. 'I'd take all that again in a heartbeat. *The Apprentice* was a brilliant experience. I was very confident that I was a capable businesswoman and it was easy to see the people who would get picked off straightaway. A lot of my most memorable moments were times when things went brilliantly or badly wrong. Trying to sell sausages in France to a halal butcher during Ramadan – priceless in terms of how wrong you can get it.

'I've learned how to let the bad stuff ride and enjoy the good stuff and that's how I've got through this year. There's only so many times you can read you are the biggest bitch in Britain and that you look like Miss Piggy before you let that stuff ride. It was a painful decision to withdraw when I'd got to the last three but I think it was the right one. At the very last minute I had to make the right decision for my children. When I watched that scene on television I could remember the tension and my mother cried watching it because she saw her daughter suffering.' Her final quip was typical of her wit. Speaking of how she pulled out of the show, the woman who has boasted of sleeping with married men said, 'This is one of the first times in my life probably that I've ever said no to a man.'

It is no surprise that Hopkins cites the France task as her memorable moment of the series, as it was without doubt one of the highlights. Getting the tasks right, and keeping the concepts fresh was the major challenge for the programme makers. 'It's the aspect of the programme that we work hardest on, and the one that gets trickier to refresh with each series,' said Kurland.

It is also the aspect of the programme in which Sugar has the most direct input. 'I have to make sure they're both doable and they're not too complex for people to follow,' he said. 'I know there are some tasks you can't do, because it would produce a boring film – like, we could get them winning and losing millions on the trading floor of a stock market, but what would you see? A bunch of people staring at screens and no viewer interest. So what we do is start off simple, and crank up the complexity as we go through.'

The France task came in Week 6 and produced hilarity

and disasters in equal measures. The task was simple: buy and sell British produce at a farmers' market in France. The team with more profit would win. Ex-British Army lieutenant Paul Callaghan led the Stealth team through a chaotic performance. He chose to buy cheap processed cheese from a British cash-and-carry, and attempt to sell that to the French of all people. They also paid over the odds for an incorrectly translated banner for their stall, and Paul then tried to cook their sausages with a makeshift tin filled with lighter fuel instead of a camping stove. Unsurprisingly, it failed to work, and Stealth lost the task. Their rivals made £410 in the task, while Paul's Stealth team lost £225. The outcome of this was inevitable: 'Paul, you're fired!'

It had been an imaginative task, and one that Sugar was proud of. He revealed that he was happy to take a bit of a lead when it came to tasks. 'Because of my marketing background, that's the one where I regard myself as a bit of an expert,' he said. 'I also like the one where they have to create a product from scratch, and we follow them as they get the components, manufacture and sell.'

Soon, it was time for Sugar to appear in the media to promote the series, although this is not likely to be a part of the job that he relishes. Never one to enjoy being interviewed at the best of times, Sugar must find the air-kissing, schmooze-fest that is the modern-day television chat show peculiarly distressing. However, he kept to his promotional duties, and his appearance on *Friday Night with Jonathan Ross* duly attracted plenty of interest even before it had been broadcast. 'Will Sir Alan Sugar fire the chat-show host?' asked *The Times*. The *Mirror*, in previewing the show, was more to the point. 'One famously hates schmoozers and the other one could schmooze for Britain, so expect Sir Alan Sugar to cut through Jonathan Ross's usual waffle like a knife through butter when he joins him on the sofa tonight.'

On the night, Sugar was on fine anecdotal form. Speaking about the trappings of his *Apprentice*-fame, he rolled out a decent yarn about a visit to a restaurant toilet. 'I was standing there trying to do my stuff and this bloke is next to me going, "Cor, that geezer was horrible in that last series." Now what they don't realise is I'm trying to get a bit of pressure up – because of my age it's a bit tricky. Anyway, it wasn't working so I zipped up. I then told my son-in-law we're going to the loo again and you're going to come and protect me.'

Asked why he thought *The Apprentice* had become such a phenomenal success, he said, 'There's an air of excitement about watching people outside their comfort zone – and there's the conflict.'

Turning to the current series' contestants, he said, 'Katie's been a tough cookie. There are loads of people like that in business, you don't have to love people, that's what the harsh commercial world is like and you have to put up with it,' he said. There was interest in the fact that he chose to defend the controversial Katie. So, what of the original Apprentice, Tim Campbell? In a typically loyal response, Sir Alan said, 'I started three years ago with the general desire to find someone to go on and flourish. Tim was very seriously underrated by the press because he didn't go out and seek publicity, he's on his own now, I say watch this space.'

Asked about rival shows, he added that he was a fan of *Dragons' Den*. 'I love it, I leap out of my chair, especially when someone brings on something electronic, I'm screaming, "Don't invest!"'

And so to the winner of Series 3: Simon Ambrose. Again, in some quarters, there was disagreement over whether Sugar had chosen the right winner. Some viewers were insistent that he should have chosen 37-year-old Kristina Grimes, who had worked as a pharmaceutical manager prior to the show and her experience was believed by many to give her the edge over the younger Ambrose. However, Ambrose was delighted to clinch the place of the Apprentice. He described himself as 'sexy, competitive, proud and ambitious' who does 'his best work under pressure'. He certainly showed many of these virtues in the tasks. As was becoming a tradition for the winner, he spoke of the example his father had set him. 'My old man was a diamond dealer and member of the London Diamond Bourse,' he said. 'He was one of the first people in jewellery discount retailing, before Ratner's; he copied the idea from a man in Newcastle. At his peak, he had a chain of shops – three of them in Oxford Street – and a factory in Birmingham. He had queues round the block when one of them opened. So a lot of my childhood was spent being dragged from shop to shop. When I was only knee-high, I remember going through darkened rooms full of boxes of 99p earrings.' He had been his own boss, with a series of Internet-related activities prior to the show. 'Being self-employed was great and I really enjoyed the freedom, but I needed a kick-start to get involved in big business and this is the way to do it. I wanted to have a real crack at something that's going to stand me in good stead to become mega-rich before I decide to settle down and spawn out loads of mini-Simons.'

He was asked if he would come good on a promise he had made to his fellow contestants that, if he won the show, he would take them all away on holiday. 'If they still want to go I'm prepared to pay for it!' he said, laughing. 'I don't think they necessarily all want to go away together, that's the problem – Tre said he'd rather be stabbed in the eye with a rusty screwdriver. I might have to take them all away individually, which is going to send me bankrupt!'

Unsurprisingly, he didn't agree with those that believed that Grimes would have made for a better winner of the show, though his reasoning gives an insight into how he sees himself. 'No, because I think he knows with someone like Kristina he'd have someone who's steadily competent, super-capable and self-sufficient. In me, he's got someone a bit more quirky, a bit more entre-preneurial, and more willing to stick his neck out and try different things. By taking on someone like that he's got to manage that. He's got to rein it in or set it free at times. So by definition he's going to have to spend more time with me, but I wouldn't have had it any other way.'

The surprise stars of the series were fast becoming not the contestants and, arguably, not even Sugar himself. Instead, his two sidekicks, Margaret Mountford and Nick Hewer, were at times stealing the show. Mountford, in particular, who had worked with Sugar for some years, was achieving a cult following among *Apprentice* aficionados. In March 1999, she was unveiled in the chairman's statement: 'Finally, I would like to take this opportunity to welcome Margaret Mountford to the board as a nonexecutive director. Margaret Mountford, a lawyer, has many years' corporate law experience as a partner in the law firm Herbert Smith, from which she retired in March 1999.' She had stood alongside Sugar throughout his ups and downs, including his legal battle with Terry Venables. It was an experience she didn't enjoy. 'That was exciting, but pretty horrible, too,' she recalled. 'The fans were ghastly. You had to go past these awful spitting yobs on the way in and out of court, which is not what one is accustomed to as a City solicitor.' However, she put up with the disgruntled fans and guided Sir Alan to the right decision. 'The court case that followed [Venables's sacking] should never have happened, it should've been thrown out. I advised Alan he was entitled to sack Venables, and I was right. But it was horrible for him, the acrimony and personal hostility he suffered – being spat at as he went to court. Some fans, in my opinion, are little better than savages. It's very tribal.'

Mountford was in the privileged position of being able to judge how much he had changed – or not – as a result of his *Apprentice*-found fame. 'He's an extremely able person. He's still very much hands-on. He hasn't been changed by fame and fortune, which says a lot about him. He has very strong family values. He's a thoroughly decent bloke and he will listen' – she inserted a telling pause – 'on occasions.'

It seems he had proved an unconventional but enjoyable client for Mountford. 'He was very different from the sort of client one had had before,' she said. 'He questions everything and never accepts things just because he's told them. He's very commercial and always holds you to an estimate. Don't give an estimate of what your fees will be if you're working for him and think you can increase them at the end.'

The admiration and respect is evidently mutual, and Sugar has had nice things to say about her too, which is something she appreciates. 'It's nice to get praise,' she said. 'Over the years I've built up a good working relationship: he knows I'll tell him what I think without worrying if he agrees or not. He doesn't like "yes" men. He's a very shrewd, clever man – so he's interesting to work with. He doesn't have small talk – he won't ask about your holiday. But he'll talk at length when he gets an idea.'

She enjoyed her work on *The Apprentice* with him and this was once more a forum where he sought and listened to Mountford's wisdom. That said, the pair did not always see the field the same way. 'We have quite a long briefing session before the boardroom . . . on who did well and who did badly. He takes our views into account. Sometimes we know who's going out – it's obvious. At other times it may be one of two – it depends on what he's looking for, whether it's someone good at sales, for instance, or a more managerial type of person. But someone whose sales technique he admires I'd probably never buy from. It's horses for courses.'

Mountford was becoming a star of the show and commentators were quick to pick up on her emerging cult status. As Anna Pickard wrote in the *Guardian*, 'Mountford's signature look is the rolling of her eyes to heaven. Indeed, most of her loudest comments about the candidates are almost entirely nonverbal. The eye-rolling is frequently accompanied by a heartfelt sigh; in extremis, a sickened pursing of the lips. Her reaction to any act of stupidity is to drop her jaw in shock and amazement. Complete idiocy causes an additional flaring of the nostrils.'

The *Irish News* also noted the many mannerisms of Mountford: 'Silver-haired with piercing blue eyes, her armoury of expressive eye-rolling and disgusted sighs has effectively ruined the chances of several candidates and her exchanges with fellow aide Nick Hewer have become some of the highlights of the series.'

Alex Clark, writing in the *Observer*, put the lawyer in a tradition of posh femininity and he liked what he was seeing. 'It's possible Margaret Mountford is the stern headmistress I never had, not coming from the kind of background that involved carpetings after high-jinks in the dorm or the battle to make the lacrosse team; it's also possible that she embodies a certain sort of female posh competence that makes the rest of us feel like we've permanently got a ladder in our tights and an uncertain grasp of Keynesian economics. Stella Rimington, Judi Dench, Stephanie Flanders (especially Stephanie Flanders) all have the same effect. Not Kirstie Allsopp, though, who attempts to carry off the same effect but looks like she might from time to time have a secret weep in a corner. Certainly, Mountford seems more suited to the task of whipping the rabble before her into shape than Sugar himself.'

In Series 4, her fame was to hit new heights when she had a nation in stitches of laughter over her comment that Edinburgh University 'isn't what it used to be'. Delivered in true dry Mountford style, this quip provoked a defensive response from the educational establishment. 'The University of Edinburgh is one of the UK's most successful and popular universities,' a spokesman said. 'It is regularly ranked among the top 50 universities in the world and is currently going through a period of unprecedented growth.' Also memorable from that series was her stunned expression when one of the candidates overcelebrated a boardroom victory.

As well as her cult status, Mountford has also become a fine example for how well women can do in business. She puts some of this down to her Ulster background. 'I think coming from Northern Ireland gives you a lot of common sense and a basic level-headedness that stands you in very good stead,' she said. 'A lot of what's required is a commonsense approach; much of business depends on that, actually. I think the basic message to give is that women have to believe in their own ability – no one else is going to believe in you if you don't believe in yourself. Though it's not the only answer to say "just go for it", if you don't go for it you're never going to get it and I think people need to be able to stand on their own feet a lot more and have more confidence in their ability. I accepted the invitation to do this because I thought it's something different. I've never had anything to do with television, it was a world I knew nothing about. I had no idea it would become so popular.

'As a City lawyer you're pretty faceless outside the clients, the accountants, those you deal with. Now, people come up to me in the street, they feel they know me. I was walking along and someone said, "That's Alan Sugar's woman." I was very innocent about it really. The recognition took me by surprise. I don't mind when people come up and say, "Who's going to win?" But sometimes they invade your personal space. Say you're in a check-in queue, there's 25 minutes of queue ahead and the person next to you says, "You're from *The Apprentice*, aren't you?" They want to stand really close and go on and on about the series. I don't like that.'

Alongside Mountford on *The Apprentice* is the simply brilliant Nick Hewer. Hewer started off in public relations during the Swinging Sixties. He formed his own PR company and quickly built an impressive client list that included the secretariat of the Aga Khan, based in Chantilly, France. He began representing Amstrad – and Sugar – in 1983. He became a trusted and valued ally for Sugar as he built his enormous business and property empire. On *The Apprentice*, he was just as vital for Sugar, and became an unlikely star in the process. As the *Independent* put it, 'With his silver, military haircut, frameless specs and deadpan intellect, Nick Hewer is not your average television star.' But he was a popular one thanks to the sharp appearance and intellect he displayed on the show.

Asked about the candidates, he was dismissive of some of them, but also found a moment of sympathy for the pressure they are under. 'I'm not sure they brief themselves that well,' said Hewer of some *Apprentice* candidates.

'Some hadn't even bothered to find out what Alan Sugar's businesses were, which was extraordinary. It's a real pressure cooker. They're working day and night. The cameras are there all the time; all their decisions are being accelerated and they don't have time to consider how to be clever. I found it tiring just watching them. Heaven knows what they must feel.'

During the lengthy filming process for each show, he is forced to spend a lot of time in their presence. Despite his respect for them, he did not become especially close to any of them. 'I don't chummy up to them,' he said. 'I think I'm considered rather sour. They try to cosy up to you, of course, but you can't afford to get friendly. You have to stand back and be impartial.'

But Hewer's fear that he is seen as 'sour' by the candidates might be misplaced. For Mrs Motormouth herself, Katie Hopkins, is most complimentary of him. 'He's a very attractive man with true charisma,' she purred. 'He knows how to talk to a woman. He once told me my lips were made for sin – but sadly I didn't get to use them on him.'

The boardroom scenes are one area where Hewer is encouraged not to be impartial, for his advice is sought by Sir Alan here. Again, Hewer feels sympathy for the candidates as the boardroom tension is racked up. 'People have been reduced to nervous wrecks,' he said. 'Sugar's got this 20-second black stare, where his pupils appear to completely dilate and they go right through you and he's just silent. It's very unnerving. And Margaret and I feel the tension, too. He doesn't tell us who he's going to fire or keep. And he's invariably got it right, over the whole series.'

Hewer's respect for both Sugar and the candidates is unflinching. With his newfound *Apprentice* fame, Hewer is often approached on the street, but anyone who wants to criticise the candidates gets short shrift from the PR guru. 'People are always saying to me, "God, what useless candidates! Where did you get them from?"' he said. 'They don't realise what enormous pressure they're under. The tasks are pretty much undertaken back to back – they're not a week apart, as they are on TV – and they go from one to the next with very little sleep, always having to watch their backs in case someone stabs them. For the fish-selling task in [Series 4], we were out at five in the morning, and went to bed around three the following morning, to be back in the boardroom at ten. They've got to have tremendous stamina.' And he should know, for he and Mountford need it too just to keep up with the candidates. 'We're on test in the tasks, too,' he explained. 'We've got to be scrupulously fair, honest and accurate. We're writing pages and pages of who said what to whom, what was the reaction, etc. Then we go into briefings with Alan and the producers that go on for three or four hours. His ability to absorb information is astounding.'

These are kind words about Sugar from Hewer, and, again, it seems Sugar reciprocates. On his own retirement,

Hewer received a wonderfully generous gesture from Sugar, who laid on a dinner at the Dorchester for Hewer and 100 invited guests. 'Sir Alan is a very generous friend,' he said. 'The best thing about working for him was there was always something going on. He has vibrancy about him.'

A lesser – but still significant – cult star of the series is Sugar's 'secretary', Frances. Sugar had a secretary called Frances Penn for many, many years, but the one you see on the screen is not, in fact, the real Frances, but an actress called Samantha Moon. Although the real Frances was not to appear in the series, as a mark of respect, her name was used for the role. Her phone calls have become a popular part of the show.

So who is the woman who plays the part of Frances? Once a receptionist at production company Talkback Thames, Moon has been playing the role since the beginning of the third series. 'Sam has always been a bit of a drama queen,' said her father Alan. 'She loved acting at school and went down to London about eight years ago with a little sack on her back determined to make it. She has met the real Frances and they got on, but Miss Penn isn't really front-of-house material. This is television and Sam fits the bill.'

Sam's mother, Gwen, says that the family were initially told to keep the truth behind her daughter's role a secret, but people began to recognise her voice and put two and two together.

Sam gets recognised on the street and feels she has to pretend that she is indeed Sir Alan's real secretary, and has become a cult figure herself in the process. One viewer wrote on an *Apprentice* fansite, 'I know the only lines she's ever delivered are "Hello" and "Sir Alan will see you now" but somehow these smoothly delivered lines are always a highlight. I'm forever waiting for the day when she will say something else. Frances makes the show for me. She's an *Apprentice* legend!'

Candidate Ghazal Asif is a fan, too, and says that he is far from alone in admiring her. 'Sam ties in with the look of the show. She is a very attractive and polished girl. She comes across as very astute. All the boys fancied her. She was almost too good to be true.'

Indeed, in Series 4, when Essex satellite engineer Simon Smith was fired, he broke with tradition to speak to 'Frances' on his way out. When she told him, 'The taxi is ready for you now,' Smith became the first candidate to say, 'Thank you, Frances.' This was typical of his old-fashioned manner. 'She's really lovely,' Smith explained afterwards. 'You go in at your lowest ebb because you've just come off the task and she always looks and smells great.'

In her role as Frances, it is Sam's job to wake up the contestants each morning for their task. 'She will get a call from the production team at 5.30am and will then have to call the candidates at the home to tell them where and when to meet for filming,' said her mother Gwen. 'Then she will do a full day's work at Talkback as a production assistant and in the evenings she will go off to do her filming for *The Apprentice*, which can last until 10pm. She will even be filming at weekends.'

But she doesn't actually meet the contestants face-to-face until they come into the boardroom to hear their fate. 'She is the first person they see then and she says they are obviously very nervous,' said her father. 'Sam has to put on this air of being a right snob, although some of the candidates still try to chat her up and give her little gifts.'

During the last series, Sam had to use her own clothes while playing the role. But this year she has been given her own allowance for outfits. 'She has to have a different outfit for each show and, as you can imagine, she has a large wardrobe now,' said her mother. 'But she doesn't get paid anything extra for doing *The Apprentice*. Her only perk is the clothing allowance.'

With even the supporting figures achieving such a popular status, *The Apprentice* was confirmed as a British television institution. Meanwhile, the true star of the show – Sir Alan Sugar – was about to cash in brilliantly on his decades of hard work.

CHAPTER NINE
INTO TOMORROW

In 2007, BSkyB bought Amstrad for £125 million. Having worked with Rupert Murdoch on the launch of Sky, and been praised warmly by the media mogul, Sir Alan Sugar was now selling his company to Murdoch. Sugar, who set up the company nearly 40 years previously and had been the leader and driving force behind its success, was pleased with the deal, which was worth £34 million to Sugar personally. (It was proving a profitable time for him. The previous month, he had sold his Tottenham Hotspur shares for £25 million.) He said, 'I cannot imagine a better home for the Amstrad business and its talented people. Our companies share the entrepreneurial spirit of bringing innovation to the largest number of customers. Sky is a great British success story. I'm proud to have worked so closely with it, and I look forward to continuing to play a part in this exciting business.'

James Murdoch of BSkyB was also delighted, saying, 'Sky and Amstrad have had a long and positive relationship. The acquisition accelerates supply chain improvement and will help us to drive innovation and efficiency for the benefit of our customers.'

Amstrad and BSkyB had indeed enjoyed a close relationship for some time, and Sugar's firm supplied around 30 per cent of the set-top boxes bought by Sky. However, he recognised that there was a vulnerability in the way Amstrad focused so much on this client. 'I turned 60 this year; I've done 40 years of hustling in this business. I have to start thinking about my team of loyal staff, many of whom have been around me for a very long time. There's a certain culture there that will exist. It's not a case of letting it go, it's a case of moving the company on to something more positive.' He added, 'The good news for my employees is that they've now got a secure future with great opportunities The bad news is that I'm still going to be around for a while, so nothing changes at Amstrad.'

That 'while' came to an emotional and powerful end when Sugar stepped down from Amstrad in 2008. 'This is a move that has been planned for a while and it's the right time for me to step down from my role at Amstrad. The past 40 years have seen Amstrad grow from a start-up business to the success story that it is today, which is credit to the talented and loyal team here. I have decided that it is the right time to step back from my role at Amstrad.'

The reins were handed to Amstrad managing director Alun Webber, of whom Sugar thoroughly approved. He said, 'Alun has worked closely with Amstrad over a number of years and is the right person to build on the success that we have seen to date. I step back knowing that the company's future is in good hands.'

On stepping down, might Sugar have begun to consider his own mortality, as many do when they retire? If not, then perhaps an event the previous year might have made him realise how fragile life can be. In July 2007, there were sensational media reports that Sugar had 'cheated death' in a 'plane-crash drama'. However, as Sugar was to reveal, the truth was somewhat less dramatic. The incident took place at the Barton Aerodrome near Manchester, on a rainy, thunderous day of weather as Sir Alan attempted to land his four-seat Cirrus SR20 private jet. This jet is noted for being the first production general-aviation aircraft equipped with a parachute for spin recovery, which can be deployed in an emergency to lower the entire aircraft to the ground safely.

'We landed at Barton, a friendly and clublike airfield now named City Airport Manchester – a far grander name than it suggests with a grass runway about the same length as a football pitch,' explained Sugar. 'We landed and ran over the end of the slippery runway by about 15 feet into some taller grass. In doing so the propeller of the plane picked up some minor damage and according to the rules this means the plane can't fly unless checked out by a qualified engineer.'

The plane was then towed by a tractor back to a hangar. Meanwhile, Sugar and his travelling companion returned to the airport clubhouse, where they were able to laugh off the incident and tuck in to a snack. 'As far as "life-threatening" is concerned, to put things in perspective my friend and I had as much chance of dying from the incident as we did in dying from food poisoning from the tuna sandwich that a very nice lady made us in the clubhouse while we waited for a mate to pick us up and take us home.'

One pilot, who was at the airfield, reportedly said, 'He wasn't shaken or hurt but he seemed quite annoyed with himself. It is only a small airport. There is not a great deal of room for pilot error. Had he been going much faster, it could have been a very different story.'

But a spokesman for Sugar tried to play the incident down. 'The accident was due to the weather being particularly wet and heavy,' the spokesman told the *Daily Mail*. 'It is also a very short runway. For Sir Alan this was just a pleasure trip. He flies a great deal at the weekends.'

Officialdom soon gave its own verdict. A report by the Air Accidents Investigation Branch into the crash on 5 July stated, 'As the aircraft turned on to the final approach, the visibility deteriorated, and the wind shifted, becoming a slight tail wind. The pilot lost sight of the far end of the runway in the poor visibility, and touched down in the middle third of runway. Conscious of the risk of skidding on the "very wet" runway, he applied light braking. The aircraft ran off the end of the runway into a rough area of long grass. Both occupants vacated the aircraft without difficulty.' The report concluded of Sugar, 'The pilot reported that, with the benefit of hindsight, he considers that a go-around would have been a safer course of action.'

Earlier that year, former newspaper editor Piers Morgan had written humorously of an in-air encounter he had with Alan Sugar. He jokingly headlined the article 'How Alan Sugar tried to kill me'. Sugar had greeted Morgan at their rendezvous at the airfield at Brentwood, Essex, with a raucous 'Oi, Morgan, you ready to die, then?' The journalist described his friend as appearing like 'Stormin' Norman Schwarzkopf in a big brown Biggles jacket and black shades'. As they belted into the plane, Sugar jokingly asked his guest whether he had made a will. All the same, Morgan had to admire pilot Sugar's flying ability, and Sugar's love of the air was palpable. 'I love it up here,' he said. 'Nobody can bother you, there are no phones or faxes or bloody emails.'

There then followed some confusion over whether another plane was in the vicinity, causing some nervous moments for the pair. As they landed, Sugar told Morgan 'I've failed . . . you're still alive!'

In the same column where he outlined his hair-raising flight with Sugar, Morgan also gave a great insight into Sir Alan and Ann's 40th wedding anniversary celebrations at their home in 2008. On arrival there, Morgan found 'a long tarpaulin tunnel patrolled by a small army of security men, leading through to an absolutely enormous marquee teeming with more than 250 people in smart black tie, standing around several large bars and gleefully guzzling vintage champagne'. The former showbiz journalist must have been to thousands of glitzy parties in his career, but this one really blew him away. 'It was spectacularly lavish, like a scene from a Corleone family wedding in *The Godfather*. The centrepiece was two giant digitally enhanced photos of the happy couple on their wedding day.'

It was a glorious evening, thoroughly enjoyed by all in attendance. The compere for the entertainment was show-business royalty Bruce Forsyth, who took to the stage with appreciative applause erupting all round. He promised 'a few surprises', and then was joined by Maureen Lipman for a foxtrot dance on the stage. 'Is that really you, Maureen?' he said, shocked when she returned to her seat. 'Oh my God, I'm so sorry!' Next on to the stage was one of Sir Alan's young grandsons, who sang the Elton John classic 'Daniel', which provoked some wry grins due to a lyric that contained the words 'Woah oh, oh, Daniel and papa, you're both as old as can be, you moan about aches and pains, now it's rubbed off on me.' And it earned the crooning youngster a deserved standing ovation. Forsyth returned to the fray, quipping, 'Sixty years in show business, and I end up being the warm-up for a seven-year-old!'

Then it was time for legendary Jewish American comedian Jackie Mason. 'I don't know why I'm here,' he joked, 'or who for, other than he's a billionaire with a big head and short legs.' By now, the guests were rolling in the aisles. But he wasn't finished. 'Sushi', he mused, 'must have been created by two Jews thinking, "How can we open a restaurant without a kitchen?"' On and on he went, with distinctly Jewish humour coming to the fore. His final quip brought the house down, and was entirely appropriate for the occasion. 'Gentiles look at Bill Gates making $100 billion and think, "Well done!" Jews think, "Is that all he makes?"'

Then the host, Sir Alan Sugar, took to the stage to a standing ovation and almost joyous respect. Speaking of his wife, he was full of love and praise. 'I can honestly say I have never ever heard anyone say a bad word about Ann,' he said. 'As you know you can't say the same about me. Talk about chalk and cheese. She always says the day she met me she knew she had met Mr Right; what she didn't know was that my first name was Always.'

He then turned to a moment in their marriage that had gained legendary status. One year, he sent his wife a birthday card, and signed it with the unbelievably inappropriately impersonal 'From Sir Alan Sugar'. Attempting to explain this to the audience, he said, 'It was a busy day in the office. Ann was not a happy bunny. So I apologised and then ran through loads of things I could buy her to make up for my mistake.'

'Do you want a new dress?' he asked.

'No,' replied his wife.

'A new watch?'

'No.'

'A car?'

'No.'

'OK, well just tell me what I can get you. To which she angrily replied, "A bloody divorce."' As laughter filled the room, Sugar added the punchline: 'I said, "Sorry, I wasn't thinking of spending that much."'

With the joking out of the way, it was time for Sir Alan to pay a more serious tribute. 'Now, ladies and gentlemen, on to a more serious and genuine note,' he said. 'I feel a bit of a fraud standing up here. It is true that over the past 25 years or so, due to my various shenanigans, the focus of attention has been on me. Quite unfairly so, as behind me is Ann – someone who has always sat in the background and let it all happen. But she has been by my side through good and bad times – fortunately not too many bad times. Ann has been a great leveller for me, and kept me on the straight and level. She, of course, wanted me to succeed in whatever I have done, but I think most of you know that's not where her priorities are.

Happy family life always came first, as well as the welfare of others.'

Sir Alan has always insisted that he not only puts his family before business, but also that this is the only way to succeed in business, by putting it second to your loved ones. It was a message he repeated on the night. 'Now here is a message to those young aspiring men here tonight. I would remind you what it is to be a successful man, and what is one's prize possession in life. It has absolutely nothing at all to do with money, academic achievement, or any material things. A real successful man puts the love of his wife and children first; a real successful man's greatest position in life is to have a great family. I am lucky enough to have had a wife for forty years, who gave me three great children, who in turn have given us seven wonderful grandchildren. You see, everything I have today is because of the love of that lady and the respect my three children have for the both of us. Ladies and gentlemen, thank you for coming, let's have a great night.'

It was indeed a great night, and one that few of those present would ever forget. Least of all Alan Sugar and his wife, who remain as happy as ever.

Once more, Sugar had shown a remarkable ability at public speaking. Many politicians would have envied his delivery for both its wit and sincerity, not least of them, the new Prime Minister, Gordon Brown. When Brown replaced Tony Blair as Prime Minister on 27 June 2007, it was a moment of excitement, fulfilment and nervousness for him. The man from Govan, Scotland, had for so long dreamed of entering Number 10 Downing Street. Having worked his way up the greasy pole of politics, he had seen his progress limited by the successful reign of Tony Blair. A rumoured 'agreement' between the pair that Brown would replace Blair was taking longer to be fulfilled than Brown wished, and relations between the pair were somewhat frosty by the time Blair finally stepped down, allowing his Chancellor to replace him as Prime Minister. The early days of Brown's reign were challenging. There was a new outbreak of foot-and-mouth disease, terrorists attacked London and Glasgow, and then there was horrendous flooding across the country. Life at the top was proving tough for Brown, and rumours that members of his own party and cabinet were plotting to replace him would have done nothing to make him feel more secure.

Not that he was without support in the country, and one of his biggest supporters was Sugar. As news spread like wildfire that Labour politicians were conspiring to replace Brown, Sir Alan emerged to back the Prime Minister. He did so in typically ebullient manner: 'You can't run a government and you can't run a company or anything like that unless everybody is on side,' he said of the plotters. His support was not merely emotional: he also offered practical tips in dealing with the detractors in the ranks. 'If they are not on side he should kick them out and then what he should do is tell the rest of the world that he has been appointed to do a job for two years and let me get on with it and then at the end of that period of time – judge me then,' said Sir Alan. He added that he felt that Brown was being unfairly scapegoated for issues that had a much more wide-ranging source. 'It's very easy for people to blame the top man when things are no good but what you have to look deeper at is what these problems are.'

These were strong words of support for Brown from one of Britain's greatest business brains. Given Brown's background and expertise in the financial side of politics, it will have meant a lot to him to hear these sentiments. And, as Sugar continued to back the embattled Scot, it transpired that his admiration was by no means a new thing. 'It's not just recently that I have backed Gordon Brown,' he said. 'I've known him for a long time as Chancellor, and I have got to know him quite well, and, out of the last four prime ministers that I have had the pleasure to have met, I think he is a very, very clever man and a man who is over everything and knows what is going on.' In what could be construed as a thinly veiled dig at the likes of Tony Blair and David Cameron, he contrasted what he saw as Brown's genuine nature, with the more theatrical, image-based politicians who dominate the 21st-century Westminster scene. 'He may not come across as some kind of actor but he has got his hand on the pulse,' avowed Sugar. At this point, it appeared he was becoming quite a commentator on the political scene, and he recalled his earliest memory of politics and the people at the top. He first became properly aware of the office of prime minister at the tender age of 15. 'It was the first time I signed on to why the country needs a leader,' he explained.

In another subtle contrast with the more showbiz politicians of the 21st century, he looked back at the political scene that dominated Britain in his youth. 'In those days a prime minister was seen as stuffy, perhaps boring, but a serious person, a person you trusted to guide the country through the challenges it faced both at home and abroad.' Clearly, Sugar saw Gordon Brown as very much in this mould. He was quick to insist that he had nothing to gain from backing Brown, no ulterior motive. 'I have no axe to grind. Let's face it, I have done OK – I am Sir Alan, recognised by the Queen for my services to business thanks to my natural-born entrepreneurial spirit. You haven't seen me up the arse of the politicians. I don't need to achieve anything or be recognised any more.'

It is little wonder that Sugar related to the fickle fortunes of politics, and how they were impacting on Brown. Because Sugar had worked in a similarly high-pressure and volatile profession – football – his heart went out to Brown as he faced schemes and behind-the-scenes machinations. 'It reminds me of my days as a football club chairman,' said Sugar. 'Walk out of the ground after giving the opponents a good hiding and the fans would chant, "Alwight, Al . . . top man . . . keep up the good work, mate . . . how's the family? . . . well done, son." A week later when we got our arse kicked, the *same* group chanted, "Oi, you tosser, what you gonna do about the team, then, eh? Get your fucking chequebook out, you fucking wanker."'

Meanwhile, *The Apprentice* was going from strength to strength. A record 20,000 applications were received for the fourth series from which 16 candidates were chosen. The contestants were housed in the Glass Factory in Battersea, and, as ever, there were plenty of characters among the 16 who made it. Raef Bjayou is a posh, handsome Exeter University graduate. He assured himself instant cult status with his pronouncements that 'the spoken word is my tool' and 'I get along with prince and pauper'. Another stand-out candidate was Michael Sophocles, the overcelebrating candidate who provoked the memorable reaction from Margaret Mountford mentioned earlier. Eccentric and a bit posh, risk manager Lucinda Ledgerwood was very much a first for the series, described by Sugar as 'zany'. It was a fair description. Then there was pin-up Alex Wotherspoon, who was a salesman with boy-band looks.

It seemed set to be a cracking series, and viewers were not to be disappointed. The second week saw both teams challenged to run an overnight laundry service. Almost inevitably, items of clothing were lost, and one team offered a 'project-manager hotline' to customers, prompting Sugar to wonder whether laundry customers would ever call a hotline 'to check on the progress of their Calvin Kleins'.

However, the most memorable tasks of the series – and one of which Sugar has expressed his pride – came when the teams were sent to Morocco to buy a list of items at as cheap as price as they could manage. This prompted comedy galore, particularly when 'nice Jewish boy' Michael Sophocles bizarrely asked a Muslim to bless a chicken for him, in order to satisfy the criteria of buying a kosher chicken. Sugar then quizzed Sophocles as to whether he was indeed Jewish, reminding him that he could always pull down his trousers to check whether he was circumcised. Eagle-eyed viewers may have noticed that Sophocles, claiming to be a 'nice Jewish boy', crossed himself prior to entering the boardroom.

The Week 11 interviews were as memorable as ever, with the addition of businesswoman Karren Brady to the panel. However, the most entertaining interviewer was, as ever, property developer Paul Kelmsley. A business sensation, Kelmsley has become a hero to aspiring millionaires across the country. On *The Apprentice*, he is always hilariously brusque with the candidates. When he reported back to Sugar in the boardroom, he noted that one candidate – Lee McQueen – had cheekily winked at him at the conclusion of the interview. As the interviewers left the boardroom, Kelmsley reprised this theme by cheekily winking at Sugar. 'Pisss offff,' responded the boss!

Not that McQueen's wink – or the revelation that he had lied on his CV – was about to get in the way of his winning the show, although he admits he was shocked himself at his victory.

'When I was told I'd won, I took a deep breath,' he said afterwards, smiling. 'I was relieved, overjoyed. My heart missed a beat. I was thinking, "Really?" Sir Alan is firm but fair. He's very, very successful and if I can take just a tiny percentage of his wealth I'll be a multimillionaire. I've got my dream job and I've already got my dream girl [his girlfriend Nicola]. I suppose now I should go down on one knee and ask her to marry me. That would really complete things, wouldn't it?

'One of the first things I'm going to have to do when I join Sir Alan's company is ask him for some time off so we can go on holiday. And I should treat Nicola to something nice like some fancy new shoes. When I was 26 I said to my mates I was going to have a Porsche 911 when I was 30. Well I'm 30 now and I've got a £100,000-a-year job so it shouldn't be long before that gets sorted.'

McQueen – who earned £75,000-a-year in his last job at Capita Group – was put in charge of a new company within Sugar's sprawling £800-million-plus empire. He explained, 'Sir Alan has bought a new business doing digital advertising and signage. I'll be running the sales teams with one of his colleagues. It's just want I wanted to do – start on something fresh and exciting.'

McQueen received fan mail galore as a result of his appearance on *The Apprentice* – from all sorts of people. 'I've had letters from gay blokes. One guy said he didn't care if I won – he just wanted to spend some time with me. I'll probably give that a miss.'

Something Sugar could not give a miss were the usual promotional rounds for *The Apprentice*. During Series 4, he was back in the interview seat at *Friday Night with Jonathan Ross* on BBC1. In what was becoming an annual outing, he once more pitched up to promote *The Apprentice* as the contestants came to the home run of their race to win the show. Once more, there was plenty of anticipation and the appearance was awarded the pick of the day in the television columns of numerous newspapers. Sitting alongside his wife Ann in the green room on the night, Sugar appeared relaxed. Ross had set up a gag during the introduction of Sugar, with comedian Alan Carr dressed up as a woman, to play the part of Frances, Sugar's 'secretary' in the series. So when it was time for Sugar to be interviewed, he phoned the green room and said, 'Frances, can you send him through?'

'Pour some Sugar on me,' sang the house-band, Four Poofs and a Piano, as Sugar appeared in the studio to rapturous applause.

Turning to the 40th wedding anniversary that Sugar

and his wife had just celebrated, Ross quipped, 'She could do better than you to be honest!'

Sugar took the banter on the chin, laughed and said, 'That's what people have always said.' Asked how he thought his wife had put up with him for 40 years, he said, 'I don't know. I think, if you knew her nature, and the type of person that she is, you'd understand how it's lasted for 40 years. She's completely the opposite to me. So, a very nice, kind caring person. But seriously, she's kept me on the straight and level.'

Ross commented how Sugar looked particularly healthy and groomed. 'I don't want to bore you with my medical history, but I had that groin problem,' said Sugar. 'They fixed it in the end. I told you the last time I was here.' He then explained how the doctor who fixed his groin had expressed disbelief that Sugar had never had a colonoscopy. What was that? wondered Ross and much of the audience. 'It's investigatory,' he said, before cutting straight to the chase by adding, 'It's when they stick a camera up your backside, you know?' He told how when the doctor had stuck the camera up, he had kept saying 'Ooh!' and 'aah!' 'I thought he'd found Lord Lucan up there!'

Turning to *The Apprentice*, when Ross asked how much control the producers had over him, Sugar was unequivocal. He denied that he was told whom to sack by the producers, and said that, other than being advised what time to turn up for filming, nobody ever told him what to do. 'I'm not an actor. Everything I say, good, bad or indifferent, comes out of my own mouth. There's no scripting.' He also praised his sidekicks Margaret Mountford and Nick Hewer as the 'unsung heroes' of the show. Then Ross showed the audience an amusing clip from a recent episode and there was laughter aplenty.

Turning from interviewee to interviewer, Sugar then decided to take control of proceedings. 'Are you going to do the *Comic Relief Apprentice*?' he asked Ross. While the host nervously pleaded with Sugar not to 'start bossing me around', the audience widely applauded Sugar's suggestion. Another of the evening's guests, Johnny Vegas, had promised to do it, added Sugar, really piling on the pressure. After Ross squirmed for a while, Sugar announced, 'So that's it, you're going to join us. You're in.' Ross agreed and they shook on it, before the host joked that Sugar would have to let him win.

Ross revealed that, in the current series of *The Apprentice*, he was very fond of Raef. 'My first reaction on seeing him was, "This man's an absolute cock,"' said Ross. 'Then by week two, I thought I rather like him!' He went on to praise Raef's sartorial elegance.

Sugar had giggled at some of Ross's comments, but he was quick to defend his man loyally. 'He's actually a very, very nice fellow. He is really a nice fellow,' said the gracious guest. He then admitted that he enjoyed firing 'evil' Jenny, because of how she turned on Sara in the boardroom and admitted he was a bit scared when he fired the other Jenny. There were then some bizarre interruptions from Vegas, who was in rather irritating mood. For reasons beyond Sugar's control, the interview never really picked up after that. However, at least he had enrolled Ross on to the *Comic Relief Apprentice*.

As it turned out, Ross's promise to appear on the *Comic Relief Apprentice* created a small headache for the show's producers. Weeks before filming on the show began, Ross landed himself in extremely hot water after a controversial appearance on Russell Brand's Radio 2 programme. The pair made some prank calls to 78-year-old former *Fawlty Towers* star Andrew Sachs, and left obscene message on the actor's phone. Soon, in part thanks to the *Daily Mail*, a media storm erupted over the matter, resulting in BBC director general Mark Thompson suspending Ross. 'He absolutely overstepped the mark,' said Thompson. 'A 12-week suspension is an exceptional step, but I believe it is a proportionate response to Jonathan's role in this unhappy affair.

'I believe that he fully understands the seriousness of what has happened. We agree that nothing like this must ever happen again and that tight discipline will be required for the future.'

However, given the charitable nature of the show, the suspension was lifted in order to allow Ross to film the *Comic Relief Apprentice*.

A show insider said, 'Jonathan was in a difficult position as his suspension came just days before filming began on the show. Pulling out at such short notice would have left producers with a headache.'

The charity spin-offs of *The Apprentice* have become a firm favourite for television viewers. *Comic Relief Does The Apprentice* was aired in March 2007, featuring a girls' team including Cheryl Cole, Jo Brand and Karren Brady and a boys' team boasting, among others, Alastair Campbell, Rupert Everett and Piers Morgan. The show had a one-off task: to run a funfair and raise funds for Comic Relief. The girls' team won the competition, but the true winner was Comic Relief, which was £1 million to the good as a result of the show. The following year, the Sport Relief charity benefited when a *Sport Relief Does The Apprentice* special was aired on BBC1. Once more the girls' team – featuring the likes of Claire Balding and Louise Redknapp – beat the boys' team, which included Nick Hancock and Lembit Opik.

The charity funds raised were a great consequence of *The Apprentice*'s success. Soon, it was time for other countries' viewers to watch the original British show and give their verdict on it. Many of the more successful reality-television shows of recent years have been imported into Britain from overseas. *Big Brother* was originally a Dutch show, and, of course, *The Apprentice* itself was an American invention. However, there are also precedents of British reality shows doing well overseas, the most striking example of which is the success of *American Idol* on Fox in the USA. The show has attracted more than 40 million viewers for its grand finale, has launched the careers of a string of stars including Kelly Clarkson, and has been described by Jeff Zucker, the chief executive of NBC Universal, as 'the most impactful show in the history of television'. However, this show that has become such a monstrous success actually came from a British original *Pop Idol*, which was launched in October 2001 on ITV. A reality music competition, it was an astonishing hit. Pop hopefuls sang in front of a panel comprising Simon Cowell, Pete Waterman, Nicki Chapman and Neil Fox. After the judging panel whittled down the contestants to a final 50, the public then voted for their 'pop idol' until the field was reduced to a final two.

And what a final two there were! Gareth Gates was a fresh-faced boy from Yorkshire with the voice of an angel when he sang, but a severe stammer when he spoke. Will Young was the posh, slightly awkward boy from Berkshire who had gathered extra support when he confronted judge Cowell about his rude and withering assessments of the contestants. The country was gripped by *Pop Idol* fever in the week of the final, and Gates and Young took to election-style campaign buses, travelling round the country whipping up support. On the night, there was an avalanche of voting and Will Young won the title. Although the second series (won by Scottish singer Michelle McManus) was less of a success, and even though *Pop Idol* has since been usurped and replaced by Cowell's new show *The X Factor*, the show's legacy and stature is for ever assured by the incredible global franchise that it has attained, with local versions of the show appearing on television worldwide from America to Vietnam.

It is in America, however, that the 'Idol franchise' has been most successful. As Ed Caesar wrote in the *Independent* on the success of *American Idol*: 'Idol has eaten America. To understand quite how gluttonously, you have to cross the Atlantic. You have to look at the newsstands, where, last week, three national magazines featured one or all of *American Idol*'s star presenters – Simon Cowell, Randy Jackson, Paula Abdul and Ryan Seacrest – on their front covers. You have to visit the supermarkets, where *American Idol* ice cream is flying off the shelves. You have to look in the record shops, where sales of *American Idol* artists have now passed 50 million units. And, of course, you have to turn on the television, where not only has *American Idol*'s prime-time slot pulled as many as 41 million viewers, but where the show's enormous reach has launched the most unlikely of stars.'

Interestingly, the success of *American Idol* has been very much credited to the team of Brits behind it: Simon Fuller, Simon Cowell, Nigel Lythgoe and Warwick. Cowell says the show has a very British sense of humour to it, and even credits the American presenter Ryan Seacrest with a 'very British' style.

With *The Apprentice*, of course, the roles were reversed: it began in America and was then imported into Britain. However, in time, the show would make the return trip as the British version was sold to America and elsewhere on the planet. Having been such a hit in the UK, it was only going to be a matter of time before *The Apprentice* was shown overseas. Given how peculiarly British Alan Sugar's gruff manner and delivery is, it was interesting to see how overseas critics would receive it, as it rolled out across the globe's television networks. It has been shown in a number of countries, including America, Australia and South Africa. In Australia, a famously plain-speaking nation, as one might imagine, Sugar's outspoken, macho delivery went down well, and there was praise aplenty for him when *The Apprentice: UK* was aired on Channel 7 in 2008. On this leading Aussie channel, the programme sat in the listings alongside shows including *Home & Away*, *Deal or No Deal*, *Make Me a Supermodel* and *10 Years Younger in 10 Days*. The channel did some imaginative marketing to promote the show in Australia, by sending attractive ladies out in Channel 7 T-shirts, handing out packets of lollipops with a sticker on the packet reading: 'Alan Sugar . . . Sweet by name, not by nature.' It was a marketing ploy that would surely have won Sugar's approval had an *Apprentice* team thought it up in one of the show's tasks.

It captured the imagination of commuters in Australia and helped create a fanbase in homes – and newspapers

– across the country. The South Australian newspaper the *Sunday Mail* led the cheers of appreciation. 'Move over Donald Trump – Alan Sugar is in the boardroom, and he's far more entertaining,' cheered their reviewer. 'The billionaire founder of 1980s electronics giant Amstrad does the firing in this UK version of the American reality show, and he's got even more chutzpah than his New York comrade (not to mention better hair). In episode one, the female contestants predictably use their sex appeal to get ahead in the challenge. The result? Sugar goes totally mental. Fantastic.' Fantastic indeed. And the hair obsession did not end with the *Sunday Mail*, with another Aussie newspaper, *The Age Melbourne*, summing up their preview of the show with, 'Sir Alan Sugar doesn't have as interesting hair as Donald Trump.'

Hair comparisons aside, Australia was falling in love with this new Cockney face on their television screens. From Perth to Sydney, Melbourne to Canberra, viewers were tuning in to see Alan Sugar's latest boardroom dressing-downs of the contestants. And they liked what they were seeing. The ringleader for the growing Sugar fan club Down Under came in the shape of the *Townsville Bulletin Australia* reviewer who summed up just why the Amstrad ace was proving such a hit: 'Overblown reality TV vehicle was self-aggrandising nonsense, but this UK version instantly caught my attention thanks to the magnetic presence of its star, Sir Alan Sugar,' he began. 'I gave Sir Alan a chance to impress . . . let's just say that he had me at, "I don't know if you're just a bloody nutter". There's an undeniably roguish charm about this latest reality TV star which makes *The Apprentice: UK* fascinating viewing. Sir Alan, however, will be a breath of fresh air to many viewers.'

The *Weekend Australian* magazine was less impressed. Placing the show in the context of the Channel 7 fortunes, it nonetheless threw a few punches. 'You can see the logic. Seven let go of the low-rating *Ramsay's Kitchen Nightmares* only to see it become a phenomenal success years later on Nine. Maybe this is another show whose time has come. But Alan Sugar, the man who founded Amstrad computing in the 1980s, does not have the sweary charm of Gordon Ramsay or, for that matter, the mercurial personality and comprehension-defying hair of Donald Trump, host of the original US *Apprentice*.' The *Sydney Morning Herald* was more positive: 'If you've seen the ads, you can easily imagine Sir Alan Sugar, the British business clone of Donald Trump, as being among the world's most unpleasant bosses. In fact, he's harsh – no doubt about that – but reasonable, too.'

The Age gave a more upbeat synopsis: '14 ambitious, congenially up-themselves swells in suits and skirts front up to the office of Sir Alan Sugar, a British self-made billionaire (in Australian dollars anyway). Sir Alan, like his US counterpart Donald Trump, has made his huge fortune through a combination of business acumen, hard work and eating people for breakfast, and here he has a smorgasbord of ego-driven, self-deluding tykes upon which to feed.'

The *Age* review continued by comparing the English version with the American original, which Aussie viewers had already enjoyed: 'There is, however, one key point of distinction. We somehow expect to see Americans tearing each other's throat out in the quest for a high-paying job, but there is still some novelty in seeing Brits doing the same thing. This becomes gloriously pronounced in the final boardroom scene where the three candidates for dismissal get sucked into a panic spiral of accusation as Sir Alan prepares to fire one of them. But the big question, of course, is: how does Sir Alan stack up compared to adorable comb-over king Donald Trump? The answer is: pretty darn well. While Sir Alan might not have the swagger of Trump's city-swallowing hubris he does have the gruff, rough-around-the-edges charm of a council-flat kid who made his pile using brains, balls and street smarts.'

So, overall, a big thumbs-up from Down Under.

As for the Americans, they were intrigued to see how their show would look and sound in the British version. As the *Newsday*, New York, newspaper put the big question: 'Does "You're Fired!" sound better with a British accent? We'll find out when CNBC imports *The Apprentice UK*. It's overseen by tough-talking business titan Alan Sugar, a working-class school dropout who made his multimillions in computers, jets and the Tottenham Hotspur football club.' Although the school dropout description was a little wide of the mark, it was clear what they were trying to do.

The *Baltimore Sun* had previewed it favourably: 'Tonight's guilty pleasure, much as I hate to admit it, I must be an Anglophile. Everything I hate about NBC's *The Apprentice*, I like in *The Apprentice: UK*, the Brit version. Self-made rich guy Sir Alan Sugar makes Donald Trump seem like a wimp.'

The CNBC channel was a fitting home for the show. It is widely regarded as the world leader in business news, broadcasting to more than 340 million homes worldwide, including more than 95 million households in the United States and Canada. It proudly launched *The Apprentice: UK* on 25 August 2008 at 9pm and 1am Eastern Time.

The reviews came thick and fast. Matt Millar in the *Daily Deal* wrote, 'On the show, which has achieved the same cult status as its US cousin, one contestant actually had the temerity to quit on camera, citing personal problems and what she insisted were other contestants' constant attempts to undermine her. Sugar gave her the evil eye and told her to shut up. Life was tough, he snarled, then fired her anyway.'

'The great thing about *The Apprentice*', wrote a columnist for the *Sun*, 'is that much as we hate most of these contestants, Alan Sugar seems to hate them far more.' Sugar, as the *Sun* columnist points out, is permanently ticked off, making Trump seem a lightweight.

The *Lansing State Journal*, Michigan, noted that the British version was more true to life than the American original: 'In this version, crusty Sir Alan Sugar does the hiring. Unlike the US version, this doesn't seem obsessed with telegenic contestants. Also, it rains a lot.'

Another feature of Sugar's post-Amstrad career has been his newspaper columns, including his must-read articles in the *Sun*. In these, he has become an articulate commentator on a number of issues, including the future of Premiership football. When Manchester City were brought by Arab billionaire Dr Sulaiman Al Fahim in 2008, comparisons were made between Al Fahim and Sugar, although these were not comparisons that Sugar necessarily went along with. 'I hear Manchester City's new owner Dr Sulaiman Al Fahim is being compared to me,' he wrote in the *Sun*. 'Well, we've both got beards, his daddy has loads of oil reserves. My daddy's reserves were in an oil can he used on his sewing machine in our council flat. And, wait for it . . . we're both doctors. Yes that's shocked you – I am a DSc from both London City and Brunel Universities. To be honest, I draw the line at hysterectomies.'

He went on to describe how he spent the transfer deadline day glued to his television screen, and was as stunned as everyone when he learned the Robinho had signed for Manchester City. However, he predicted trouble ahead at the club, between their new owner and manager Mark Hughes. 'I have visions of Dr Al calling a meeting in the dressing room: "Hello and greetings . . . Mr Mark, I don't like this 4–4–2. We play next week Camel formation, OK, do it."'

Returning to his infamous 'Carlos Kickaballs' statement of the 1990s, Sir Alan claimed to be vindicated. 'We wonder why we can't put out a good England team. The reason is the Premier League attracts all the imports – as I put it 15 years ago, the Carlos Kickaballs who have no interest in the UK club they play for. They are playing for themselves. This is stopping young English players getting a chance to enhance their skills and learn their trade in the teams that they really love and admire. Teams they really did follow as a boy.'

So Sugar remains as sharp as ever when dissecting the football world, but the topic where it seems he is at his most eloquent and powerful is that of politics. In 2008, he was quick to pounce on an own goal by Conservative leader David Cameron, who had moaned about *The Apprentice* and its star, saying, 'I can't bear Alan Sugar. I like TV to escape.'

On hearing of this Cameron putdown, Sugar had an immediate and witty riposte: 'I'm glad he can't bear me. Perhaps he will stop asking people to sound me out if I want to meet him and defect to his party.' He added, 'I am still waiting for him to answer my question: if he was in power would things be any different? He seems to know when to stay silent.'

Everyone seemed amused at Cameron's cock-up. The *Mirror* wrote, 'Novice David Cameron committed a schoolboy howler by getting into a slanging match with Sir Alan Sugar. When Mr Cameron comes out of hiding next week he must come up with answers to the vital questions. And Sir Alan will be there to shout: 'You're fired!'

The *Sun* echoed the sentiment, 'Sugar and spite: Sir Alan exposes Tory Leader Cam as a sham'.

Sugar was very impressed with Gordon Brown for his handling of the banking crisis. 'It seems the Prime Minister has been very smart, as yesterday the Americans announced an almost carbon copy of his plans,' wrote Sir Alan. 'However, with all that banking stuff sorted, we have to consider ongoing issues. We are not out of the woods yet.' The main ongoing issue Sugar suggested we focus on was simple: buy British. 'I would never have thought I would be dishing out compliments to the French, but there are some things I admire about them. Chief among them was that the French public made a patriotic effort to buy French.'

He urged, via the pages of the *Sun*, the British public to do likewise. Naturally, it was a campaign that truly captured the imagination of the *Sun* readers.

Even *Dragons' Den* Dragon James Caan put aside seeming TV rivalries and backed the Sugar-led campaign. He wrote, 'I want to back the *Sun*'s campaign to support small businesses but would argue a package for stimulation could go even further. We are a nation of shopkeepers and somehow Government support for our nation has dwindled and with it confidence that things will get better. At a time when small businesses need to be springing to life, instead so many obstacles are in their way.

'During the last recession in 1992, after a year of hard work I was left with a profit of £1,500 for my recruitment business. The year before it had made £450,000, so I know a recession is very challenging. But this is different, because in my 25 years of business I have never had to question the survival of a bank. I have gone to the banks with a very credible business and they have said they have no money to lend.

'So in a situation where banks are refusing to lend and a small business needs more money, my best advice is to cut costs. If your cost base is higher than your income, you are heading in the wrong direction. When you have gone through a buoyant economy most businesses have monthly expenditure commitments which are not nice to have. They should reduce them.'

It was not just the great and the good of business and television who echoed Sugar's 'buy British' plea: so too did ordinary *Sun* readers. As one reader wrote, 'Sir Alan Sugar couldn't be more right. I found his article truthful, hard-hitting and very supportive towards the

British public. The Government should take a leaf out of his book.' Another added, 'I agree with Sir Alan and support British industry. I own a small recruitment business built from my bedroom over ten years. In the past year I've lost six of 15 staff. It is very hard.' Yet another suggested simply, 'Sir Alan should run for Mayor of London.'

Soon, he was being put forward for an even greater job. In 2008, it was revealed that many Brits believe Sugar would make the ideal Prime Minister. The *Apprentice* tycoon topped a poll to find the 'dream cabinet'. In the poll of 3,000, actor Stephen Fry was Deputy PM, while outgoing *Countdown* queen Carol Vorderman became Chancellor and U2's Bono and explorer Michael Palin jointly led the Foreign Office. Terry Wogan was Home Secretary, Gordon Ramsay got Health and Jeremy Clarkson Transport. It sounds like quite a Cabinet!

Still, the fickle nature of fame was spelled out clearly when, soon after being 'voted' Prime Minister, Sugar failed to make the *Jewish Chronicle*'s Jewish Power 100. One judge, Ben Rich, explained how the list was compiled. 'It's not about famous Jews. Otherwise we would have Amy Winehouse. Sir Alan is a generous philanthropist, but does not pursue a specific agenda. However, his recent comments about kosher chicken may indicate he wants to.' One would hope so: there are few more powerful Jews in Britain than Sir Alan

Sugar, who was ranked 92nd in the *Sunday Times Rich List* in the same year the *Jewish Chronicle* chose to overlook his achievements.

But let us return to the boy who set out on this extraordinary business journey, back in the 1960s. He had watched his father slog hard for other people, too weighed down by family responsibility to strike out alone in business. Alan Sugar was not about to follow that example. Once he was up and running in business, he employed his father. After he had done so, the differences in their approach to life were highlighted as starkly as ever. 'I wanted to stop him working for the old sweatshops,' explains Sugar of his decision to employ his old man. 'He was earning something like £20 a week in the garment business, and the way I was doing business, 20 quid a week was nothing. So he might as well come and work for me and answer my telephones and wrap a few parcels up. He was much happier doing that than being under the constant threat of having no work in the sweatshops.

'When he had to tie up parcels, he would stroll around the nearby market looking for pieces of string that people had dropped, to save money on string. He would recycle postage stamps to save money when invoicing customers. "Dad, do me a favour – we can afford stamps." After all, these invoices were for tens of thousands of pounds, so why worry about the pennies that a stamp would cost?'

As Sugar's fortunes grew, he bought new homes and, as his parents visited him in his grand homes, their jaws would drop. 'They were totally confused,' he said. 'They couldn't take it in. They just hadn't realised how big Alan had got.'

Sugar spent years persuading them to move out of their flat in Hackney, and into a nicer flat in Redbridge. He bought them holidays in Israel and America, but felt he had to pretend that the first-class tickets he had bought them had been given to him as a gift, so they wouldn't feel he had been too extravagant.

His parents have both died now, but they must have been extraordinarily proud of their remarkable son. A loving family man and business genius, Sir Alan Sugar should make every Brit proud to come from the same shores as he has. Indeed, you really would need a heart of stone not to be moved and utterly awed by the success that Sugar has made both of his business and personal life. He was an outsider, but never let his lack of establishment acumen get in his way. Indeed, if anything, Sugar made a virtue of his background. This giant success story was the rebel of the financial world, and he also revolutionised the high street and the home with his electrical products.

The boy from Hackney who became a multi-millionaire, television star and inspiration to budding entrepreneurs everywhere, Sir Alan Sugar is an example to us all for the way he has conducted his life. Dubbed 'probably Britain's greatest entrepreneur' by none other than Rupert Murdoch, he is so much more than that. A national treasure and star in every sense of the word, the business giant might put on a grumpy front on *The Apprentice*, but do not let that fool you. For Sir Alan Sugar really is as sweet as they come.

Here ends the latest chapter of his story, but there is surely more to come from Alan Sugar. Not least because he believes that even a man as successful as he is never stops learning.

'I'm not claiming to know it all, and don't ever call me a business guru because I'm still learning,' he said humbly. 'It may sound like a cliché, but I learn something new every day.'

And his advice to anyone wishing to be the next Sir Alan Sugar? 'Take stock of what you're doing. Keep an eye on the profit, because people lose track of that. The costs can run away with themselves. There's no point making cakes that people love, and selling loads of them at £5 a cake, if they're costing you £7 to make.'

Sugar has an estimated fortune of £830 million, but he insists there are far more important things in his life. 'It's only money. What you have to worry about in life is that your loved ones and the people close to you are healthy and well. It's just money. If I lost it all tomorrow I would go and make some more. So what? It is not my God.'

BIBLIOGRAPHY

Sugar, Alan, *The Apprentice – How To Get Hired, Not Fired* (BBC Books, 2005).

Thomas, David, *Alan Sugar – The Amstrad Story* (Century, 1990).

AKNOWLEDGEMENTS

Thanks to Stuart Robertson, John Blake and
Lucian Randall.